DATA TEAMS

Success
STORIES

VOLUME 1

DATA TEAMS

Success
STRIES

VOLUME 1

KRISTIN R. ANDERSON

**LEAD+
LEARN
PRESS**

ENGLEWOOD, COLORADO

The Leadership and Learning Center
317 Inverness Way South, Suite 150
Englewood, Colorado 80112
Phone 1.866.399.6019 | Fax 303.504.9417
www.LeadandLearn.com

Published by Lead + Learn Press, a division of Advanced Learning Centers, Inc.

Library of Congress Cataloging-in-Publication Data:

Anderson, Kristin R.
  Data teams success stories / Kristin R. Anderson.
    p. cm.
  Includes bibliographical references.
  ISBN 978-1-935588-01-6
  1. Educational tests and measurements--United States. I. Title.
  LB3051.A697 2010
  371.26--dc22
                                    2010025782

ISBN 978-1-935588-01-6

Printed in the United States of America

14 13 12 11 10   01 02 03 04 05 06 07

Contents

About the Author

Kristin R. Anderson began her career as a high school English teacher for students who were kicked out of Denver Public Schools. Since then, she has worked in multiple K–12 settings in various administrative roles, and has obtained advanced degrees from Sterling College in Kansas, the University of Denver, and the University of Colorado at Colorado Springs. She is a longtime student of the field, a passionate educator, and an inspirational leader. Kristin is currently Senior Director of Professional Learning with The Leadership and Learning Center in Englewood, Colorado, and resides in Castle Rock with her husband and two children.

Acknowledgments

Thank you to the following people who made this book happen; for telling your stories in the hope that they will transform old thinking and archaic ways, and will help schools, districts, and departments of education create a new culture—one that is defined by empowered educators and engaged students, and that results in high student achievement.

- Olwen E. Herron, Ed.D.—Chief Accountability and Organizational Development Officer, Fort Bend Independent School District, Sugar Land, Texas

- Dr. John R. Hill—Director of Curriculum and Instruction, Elkhart Community Schools, Elkhart, Indiana

- Brady T. Wald, M.Ed.—Assistant Principal, Gililland Middle School, Tempe, Arizona

- Jennifer Wildman—Principal, Landmark Elementary School, Watsonville, California

- Koleen Lorenzana—Language Arts Teacher, Edison Middle School, Edison School District, Bakersfield, California

- John Van Pelt, Ed.D.—Superintendent, Lake Villa School District 41, Lake Villa, Illinois

- Jeffrey Keller—Principal, Marylin Avenue Elementary School, Livermore, California

- Dolores Garcia-Blocker, Ed.D.—Principal, Cooperative Arts and Humanities Magnet High School, New Haven Public Schools, New Haven, Connecticut

Thank you as well to the many courageous educators behind these stories: members of the Data Teams, the schools' support staff members, and the administrations that made brave decisions to change schedules, invest in professional development, and go against the flow. As a Native American proverb states, "It takes a thousand voices to tell a single story."

Finally, thank you to the two Krises in my life who inspire me to live each day to the fullest. Kris Wagner, my mom, who has always believed in me and told me I can do anything I put my mind to, and Kris Anderson, my husband, who has supported me in all my endeavors, whether crazy or worthwhile—I can't imagine anyone I would rather write the story of my life with.

Introduction

Throughout history, storytelling has been one of our most respected art forms. This medium transcends race, time, sex, and religion. In fact, cultures are defined by the stories behind them. In the words of Chris Cavanaugh, "Storytellers, by the very act of telling, communicate a radical learning that changes lives and the world: telling stories is a universally accessible means through which people make meaning."

Stories can be told orally or through photographs, print, charm bracelets, scrapbooks, and so on. Here are examples of stories that have changed lives and defined cultures:

- Rosa Parks' refusal to give up her bus seat to a white man indirectly led to some of the most significant civil rights legislation in the United States. Her choice to create a new chapter in a story deeply ingrained in the culture of the American South earned her a place in history as one of the most well-respected figures in the civil rights movement, and inspired bravery and confidence in African Americans and women across the nation.

- Anne Frank's diary is one of the most widely read books in the world. It reveals the thoughts of a young, yet surprisingly mature, 13-year-old girl, confined to a secret hiding place during the Holocaust. She taught future generations the power of belief and hope through her enduring words, "Despite everything, I believe that people are really good at heart."

- Joanna Rowling's work was rejected by many publishers. When the first edition of the first Harry Potter novel was finally published, the print run was only 1,000 copies. She was advised to disguise her feminine identity, and published her books under her initials: "J. K." Although people initially thought of her ideas as outlandish, she is now internationally revered for her creativity and storytelling ability. Her fan clubs have thousands of members who continue to live out and carry on her story.

Culture has been defined as:

- "A set of common understandings around which action is organized…finding expression in language whose nuances are peculiar to the group," (Becker and Geer, 1960).

- "A set of understandings or meanings shared by a group of people that are largely tacit among members and are clearly relevant and distinctive to the particular group, which are also passed on to new members," (Louis, 1980).

- "A system of knowledge, of standards for perceiving, believing, evaluating and acting . . . that serve to relate human communities to their environmental settings," (Allaire and Firsirotu, 1984).
- "Any social system arising from a network of shared ideologies consisting of two components: substance—the networks of meaning associated with ideologies, norms, and values; and forms—the practices whereby the meanings are expressed, affirmed, and communicated to members," (Trice and Beyer, 1984).

Data Teams, created by The Leadership and Learning Center in 2001, exemplify all four of these definitions.

- The Data Teams process is a model for continuous, collaborative action that inspires and empowers professionals to improve teaching, learning, and leadership for *all*.
- Data Team meetings are structured around a systematic step-by-step process (collect and chart the data, make inferences, establish SMART goals, determine strategies to address the goals, and monitor the progress/results).
- Data Teams adhere to continuous improvement cycles, examine patterns and trends, and establish specific timelines, roles, and responsibilities.
- Data Teams provide relevant, formative data, and are aligned with high-stakes assessments to provide the greatest leverage point for accountability and improvement.

Melody Beattie said, "Live your life from your heart. Share from your heart. And your story will touch and heal people's souls." We all know that educating children is, indeed, meaningful work. It is our passion, drive, inspiration, and desire to change the world that keep us motivated to stay the course, even during times of great frustration and chaos. While we may live our educational lives from our hearts, because leading, teaching, and learning is harder work than most anyone can imagine, we unfortunately rarely take the time to share our stories. We feel like all the stars have aligned if we are able to plan lessons a few days in advance, if our grades are current in the grade book, and if all of the required reports are turned in.

The book you are about to read is a collection of stories told by your peers in the industry. They are ordinary people—superintendents, principals, and teachers—many of whom have never written a newspaper or magazine article, let alone a book. What could be more exciting than experiencing living history?

No story changes the lives of its readers unless they commit to careful reflection, thought, analysis, and application. The reflection pages that immediately follow each story are titled "Writing My Success Story." They serve as a venue for you to process the messages, deliberate practices, and courageous decisions of each school or district represented in this book as they implemented Data Teams. Feel free to write, draw, and plan on these pages and consume this publication; use it as a tool to help you refine, construct, and create your educational legacy.

Maybe you're in a place right now where you could use some inspiration, a different lens to look through, or a new way of thinking. Perhaps you just need to be encouraged by the tale of someone in your position who has been able to implement and sustain great change. Or maybe you are from a school or district that has good results, and does well consistently, but which has also become stagnant or complacent. This book is for all of you: those who are struggling; those who are discouraged; those who are stuck in a rut; and those who continuously push themselves to grow, learn, and improve. I hope this book helps you achieve the success you desire, and create the culture that you hope will endure in your school.

SUCCESS STORY ONE

Cooperative Arts and Humanities Magnet High School, New Haven, Connecticut

"The Data Teams process is at the core of my belief system for improving student achievement, not only for struggling students, but for the students who are functioning at high levels as well."

—Dolores Garcia-Blocker, Principal

SUCCESSFUL CLIENT:	Cooperative Arts and Humanities Magnet High School
LOCATION:	New Haven, Connecticut (Urban)
POPULATION:	550 students
AUTHOR:	Dolores Garcia-Blocker, Ed.D., Principal

This story is about the steps we followed at Cooperative Arts and Humanities High School to implement the Data Teams process in our school. Our implementation of the Data Teams process continues to be a work in progress. We do not have a "magic formula," but we'd like to share some best practices that worked for us, which other schools or districts might find useful.

As the school principal responsible for leading this process, and because this continues to be a *team* process, I have written this chapter with input from others at the district office level as well as the administrative and teacher leadership levels within our school building. Our hope is that, in reading our story, you will find something that will assist you in the implementation of a Data Teams process in your own district or school.

School Description, Demographics, and Test Data

Cooperative Arts and Humanities High School, which we call Co-Op, is a visual and performing arts magnet school in New Haven, Connecticut. Students come to Co-Op through a lottery process. They apply to one of seven art departments (visual arts, dance, theater, creative writing, instrumental band, instrumental strings, or choir) and hope to get in through a lottery that is held every spring to determine the entrants for the following school year. Sixty-five percent of the students reside in the city of New Haven, while 35 percent reside in one of nineteen neighboring towns.

We are one of two full-time visual and performing arts high schools in the state of Connecticut. The students who come to Co-Op commit to studying their chosen art discipline for 25 percent of the day for four years. We have a comprehensive college preparatory academic and arts program that prepares students for the global competition to get into college that they will face as seniors.

Our school's recent enrollment information is listed in Figure 1.1, and our student demographics for the 2009–2010 school year are in Figure 1.2.

FIGURE 1.1

Enrollment		
2008–2009	**2009–2010**	**2010–2011**
450 students	550 students	650 students

FIGURE 1.2

2009–2010 Demographics

Black	White	Hispanic	Asian
49%	26%	23%	4%

Female	Male
70%	30%

Free/Reduced Lunch	Special Education	English Language Learners
65%	6%	2%

In Connecticut, under the No Child Left Behind Act, we administer the Connecticut Academic Performance Test (CAPT) to all tenth graders statewide. Figure 1.3 shows our school data from that test for the past four years in math, reading, writing, and science. The numbers represent the percentage of students who scored at the proficient or better level on each of the assessments.

FIGURE 1.3

	2006	2007	2008	2009
Math	55%	62%	50%	64%
Reading	73%	67%	68%	89%
Writing	78%	84%	85%	92%
Science	69%	70%	65%	64%

Implementation of Data Teams in New Haven Public Schools

About three years ago, district-level administrators mandated that the Data Teams process be implemented in all schools in the district.

Charles Williams, Director of High Schools, says of the process, "Early on, while the use of data to determine classroom practice was a fledgling idea in the district, Dr. Garcia-Blocker and her school team decided that student data would be the formal approach to lesson design, initiation, and assessment. This process has become a living document in the daily, weekly, and yearly declaration of student progress. Dr. Garcia-Blocker and her staff have centered their work on research-based practices through the work of the building Data Team and the expert tutelage of Dr. Connie Kamm, a consultant from The Leadership and Learning Center. They now stand as exemplars in the district and the state as we move forward in our efforts to provide a learning environment that optimizes the educational mastery of each student."

From the beginning, our district provided all of its schools with high-quality professional development targeted at different levels (administrators, lead teachers, classroom teachers, departments, and grade levels). I made sure that Co-Op took advantage of everything the district offered. The key to the success of the district's professional development and support plan is that it is ongoing, and is differentiated depending on the needs of each school.

At Co-Op, we had the good fortune of regularly working with Dr. Connie Kamm, a Professional Development Associate from The Leadership and Learning Center. She mentored me, and guided the administration and faculty through the process of developing and implementing Data Teams at the building, department, and course levels. The professional development was differentiated, because everyone was at varied levels of understanding and implementation. More importantly, when we sent our Data Team meeting minutes, unit plans, Common Formative Assessments, and other documents to Dr. Kamm, we were given immediate and very specific feedback about our strengths, weaknesses, and next steps.

Imma Canelli, Assistant Superintendent of Curriculum and Instruction, says, "It has been a very rewarding experience watching Dr. Garcia-Blocker and her leadership team implement the Data Teams process at Co-Op. As a district, we have been providing professional development through seminars by The Leadership and Learning Center such as Data-Driven Decision Making, Making Standards Work, and Common Formative Assessments. We have also provided technical support to schools to help them establish building leadership Data Teams as well as academic/content Data Teams. Co-Op High School, under the leadership of Dr. Garcia-Blocker, has embraced this professional development and is the flagship high school in our district. We are really proud of the hard work Co-Op has done in developing Common Formative Assessments, analyzing data, and providing appropriate instruction to meet students' needs. I have never seen a leadership team so dedicated to the process. It is infectious. Their hard work has paid off in just two short years—Co-Op achieved adequate yearly progress this past school year."

The Culture at Co-Op High School

The Data Teams process is at the core of my belief system for improving student achievement, not only for struggling students, but for the students who are functioning at high levels as well. Data Team meetings are not about the students, but rather about what the adults commit to do to address the students' needs as identified in the data.

I became a real believer in this process when our district's officials brought in the superintendent of another Connecticut school district to speak with building administrators about how he used the Data Teams process in his school district to raise student achievement at all levels in grades K–12. His story was so inspiring that it motivated me to fully commit to implementing the Data Teams process at Co-Op at the building, department, and course levels.

In order to bring this process to the teachers at Co-Op, it had to be embedded in the culture of the school. I had to see and approach this endeavor as a *process*, and develop an implementation plan that slowly built internal leadership capacity, starting with the school administrators and lead teachers.

"It has been an educational experience for me to support the dedication and commitment of Dr. Garcia-Blocker and her entire leadership team," says Donna Aiello, Director of Professional Development. "They have embraced the practice of using the school Data Team to analyze data, reflect on teaching and learning, and design tier two indicators (in relation to district goals) and they have accepted the challenge of creating a culture that focuses directly on School Improvement Plan goals and, at the same time, addressing the individual needs of all students."

John Laub, a lead teacher at Co-Op, says, "As a huge sports fan, analyzing statistics and data always intrigued me, so recording and examining student data came rather easily. As the social studies department head at Co-Op, I compile data at all levels: college, honors, and advanced placement. Data guides department decisions across the curriculum and allows us to dig deeper into teacher account-ability and student performance. It is now the essential tool in our teaching cache. I can't imagine moving forward without using data to make key decisions."

Professional Development

I felt it was very important to slowly build capacity within the leadership team to make sure this process took hold in the building. The sole focus of most faculty meetings and *all* in-service days has been, and will continue to be, deepening our understanding of the Data Teams process. Each faculty meeting or in-service day has as its focus one or two very specific areas of the Data Teams process (e.g., establishing roles, recording or analyzing data, selecting instructional strategies). It is easy to lose focus because of the many things school administrators face as we do our jobs; faculty meetings and in-service days become wasted opportunities if they are filled with "administrivia." I often hear administrators complain that there is no time to do "this stuff" (professional development). Having a clear and focused plan for faculty meetings and in-service days—and not wavering from that plan—will give administrators considerable opportunities throughout the year to provide professional development to the entire faculty. Keeping the teachers focused on the Data Teams process has been my priority and primary focus for all in-school professional development.

Lead Teacher Structure

In order to successfully implement the use of Data Teams school-wide, I established a lead teacher structure in our school. Understanding that the "work" of the Data Teams process is done as a *team* is a fundamental reason for having a team of teacher leaders. Administrators cannot lead this work by themselves. We must identify a team of teachers who will carry the message and will lead the process in their respective departments.

Our building-level Data Team is made up of all the lead teachers from the academic and art departments, support services, and administration (Figure 1.4).

FIGURE 1.4

Building-Level Data Team Representatives

Academic	Arts	Support Services	Administration
English	Visual Arts	Guidance	Principal
Math	Music (band, strings, and choir)	Special Education	Assistant Principals
Science		Honors/Advanced Placement	
Social Studies	Dance		
Languages	Theater		
	Creative Writing		

All of the lead teachers have a common planning time within the school day. Because we have a modified block schedule at Co-Op, the building-level Data Team has a standing weekly one-hour meeting. We also have the ability to meet twice weekly for 90 minutes and once for 45 minutes, if needed.

Building-level Data Team member Fallon Daniels, the Co-Op's lead teacher in science, says, "Our building-level Data Team and lead teacher structure is an exemplary indicator of school reform, in the sense that we are moving from a traditional school organization to a twenty-first century school organization that recognizes the importance of human capital among the staff, and supports the staff through learning, collaboration, and consensus. In addition, we promote building individual student performance through the analysis of data from various forms of assessments to measure individual growth."

Lead teacher Andrea Sauerbrunn says, "Representing the special education department in our building-level Data Team has given me the opportunity to collaborate with lead teachers to standardize and unify the accommodations and modifications of curriculum for students with special needs at all grade levels and in all disciplines. This has ensured that the implementation of individualized educational programs throughout the building is synthesized with district and state standards."

Common Departmental Planning Time

The successful functioning of any school is very much tied to scheduling. It is imperative that the principal be involved in scheduling for the building—preferably *directly* involved. Administrators must approach the scheduling of a school with an overall philosophy in mind, and the schedule should reflect the top priorities of the school.

As I scheduled Co-Op, my first priority was making sure teachers had time within the school day to conduct their Data Team meetings. The success of the Data Teams process relies on a schedule in which departments and grade levels have common planning times built into the school day. Including common planning time in the schedule guarantees that teachers have time within each week to meet on a regular basis. Expecting teachers within a department, course, or grade level to grab time from lunch, before or after school, or during breaks will not work; the level of conversation, sharing, planning, etc. that needs to happen during Data Team meetings requires formal scheduled meetings.

According to lead English teacher Dina Secchiaroli, "Using the scheduled common planning times to have Data Team meetings has been vital to our success as a department. Because we've been working together so often and for so long, our teaching has become much more cohesive. We communicate much more effectively: using the same language, knowing the skill sequence we need, remembering what worked previously and what needed to be adjusted. Consequently, our teaching has become much more transparent, and our Data Team meetings have become much more succinct and effective. What used to take us eighty minutes or more to do now takes us anywhere from fifteen minutes to forty minutes, depending on whether we're talking about something new or revisiting a skill to refine our instruction. Not only have *we* noticed a difference, but the students have also articulated that the learning they receive from different teachers and departments is more consistent."

Modeling and Monitoring

Some of the keys to successful lesson planning and delivery are continuous modeling and monitoring. Ensuring the proper implementation of the Data Teams process required me to make sure the various elements of the process were continuously modeled and properly monitored.

I created and provided the teachers and Data Teams with templates, which have since been modified a few times based on teacher recommendations, to help them gather, record, and report their data, findings, and plans to address student needs that emerge from the data. These templates ensure that the same questions are being answered at all Data Team meetings, and it allows for all meeting minutes to be reviewed similarly by the building-level Data Team. Below are the six questions, at a minimum, the teachers *must* answer at each Data Team meeting:

1. What are the students doing well?

2. What are the students *not* doing well?

3. What is the *specific* plan to address the area(s) in which the students are not doing well? In addition, what is the *specific* plan to address the needs of the students who are already proficient?

4. What is the evidence that the strategy is being taught (adult actions)?

5. What is the evidence that the strategy is working (student outcomes)?

6. What is the date by which the effectiveness of the strategy will be assessed?

All Data Team meeting minutes must be submitted to the building-level Data Team for our review and monitoring. Our school district now requires that the minutes be posted on the school's Web page. An additional built-in monitoring mechanism is my requirement that the supervising administrator be present at all Data Team meetings he or she supervises.

One practice the building-level Data Team has implemented this year is the monthly monitoring of our School Improvement Plan. Our School Improvement Plan is a living document that the building-level Data Team reviews at one of our monthly meetings. At the moment, we are monitoring to make sure all of the department and course Data Teams are meeting at least twice monthly. All teams are meeting to review, discuss, and plan for the instructional needs of the students as they relate to writing within the discipline and one other content-specific skill (e.g., art critiques, music theory, science inquiry, English text analysis, etc.).

Chris Cozzi, the lead teacher in visual arts, says "As professionals, we each approach the art of teaching in our own unique way. The Data Teams process has put us all on the same page, creating a format that enables us to communicate specifically and address inadequacies in our methods with concrete, measurable solutions."

Hiring Practices

One of the greatest legacies of a principal is the faculty (including administrators) he or she hires. Because the hiring and eventual tenure-granting decisions impact the culture of the school long after the principal is gone, principals have to be mindful of the teachers they hire. We must take this part of our practice very seriously. Teachers will either support or undermine a school's vision or culture, including its effective use of the Data Teams process.

I have had the opportunity to hire more than 90 percent of the teachers at Co-Op. In every interview, teacher candidates are asked to discuss their understanding of (brand new teachers) or experience with (veteran teachers) the Data Teams process to see if they would be a good fit at Co-Op. Because the success of the process relies on the teachers, it is important to hire only teachers who support the process. Teachers who neither understand nor support the Data Teams process are not hired to teach at Co-Op.

Alicia Thompson, a lead algebra teacher in her first year at Co-Op High School, says, "I have had the opportunity to lead Data Team meetings at Co-Op as well as outside of Co-Op. Working with teachers who have similar mindsets about the impact that data analysis can have makes an enormous difference in the type of meeting that is held. When there is even one teacher who refuses to see the benefits of data-driven instruction, meetings take longer, cause tension, and provide little or no benefit to students or staff. However, when a group of teachers is willing to use relevant data to improve teaching practices, the Data Teams process yields positive results in student learning."

Notable Changes at Co-Op Due to the Data Teams Process

During the 2008–2009 school year, the leadership team at Co-Op committed to redefining our purpose by focusing on the implementation of a strong building-level Data Team. Throughout that year, we were steadfast in reviewing and analyzing our state test data from previous years, implementing school-wide and content-specific instructional plans based on that data, and then monitoring and adjusting those plans based on ongoing data collection. As a result, our Connecticut Academic Performance Test (CAPT) data gains in reading and math (which were our areas of focus) for that year was the most impressive data we have had throughout the history of the test's administration at our school (see Figure 1.3). Below are some of the things the building-level Data Team felt we did really well that year to net those results:

- We analyzed the information from Common Formative Assessments to identify school-wide patterns and strategies to address common needs (e.g., quote attack strategy).

- We created and implemented a "CAPT Staycation" that involved daily, fun, small-group and grade-wide activities for the students in school and in the downtown area after they took the CAPT.

- We refined the selection process for the students targeted for the three-week "CAPT Academy" in February.

- We maintained open communication with the students throughout the months leading up to the CAPT, so that they really became partners in the process.

- We maintained a partnership with all departments—everyone "owned" the CAPT performance of our students and worked in a collegial manner for the common good of the school.

- We familiarized students with the CAPT assessment and its language.

- We familiarized students with the CAPT scoring rubrics, so that they clearly understood what they needed to do to "pass" the test.

Teacher Commitment to the Process

As the years have gone by, teachers are getting better at working in Data Teams. In particular, there is a marked difference in the conversations and planning for student growth in the arts. Now there is a greater willingness to collaboratively review student work, develop scoring rubrics, and plan for the instructional needs of the students. There was some initial resistance to the Data Teams process among the arts faculty, but I believe that resistance was due to the arts faculty viewing "data" as "numbers"—something quantifiable—instead of simply as student work. The arts faculty's next task is to define what "proficiency" and "mastery" look like in their respective disciplines. This will help to clarify the language in their rubrics, which, in the end, should help students understand specifically what they need to do to advance to their next level of artistry.

Lead music teacher Patrick Smith says, "My colleagues in the music department and I have found that the Data Teams process has helped us to identify trends in our overall student development, giving us concrete verification of our musical suspicions. The major benefit, however, is the common planning time that the Data Teams process requires. Our level of inter- and intra-departmental communication has improved significantly as a result."

Reflections on Our Future

Our next level of work with the Data Teams process at Co-Op will be in the area of understanding high-leverage, research-based instructional strategies. As I review the Data Team meeting minutes from all departments, I have found that the teams are really good at identifying what students are doing well and what the students are not doing well. However, when it comes to the development of a plan to address the students' needs instructionally, the teams are listing activities, rather than strategies.

I will be developing a one-year professional development plan for implementation during the upcoming school year focusing on instructional strategies. I truly believe that this will make a marked difference in our building, department, and course Data Team meetings, and, ultimately, will increase student achievement in all areas.

Lead creative writing teacher Judi Katz offers the following observations about using Data Teams: "At its best, the Data Teams process is deeply collaborative, and collaboration is difficult. Everyone likes to think they are good collaborators, but what they generally mean is that they are good at figuring out what they think needs to happen and then convincing others to do it. That is not collaboration. Collaboration actually involves a lot more listening and a lot less talking than most educators are used to. We are asked to answer six specific questions when we meet in our Data Teams. In creative writing, it seems, we always end up asking ourselves the following four more. As teachers:

- What did we do well?
- What didn't we do well?
- How can we capitalize on what we did well to move each student or group of students to the next level of proficiency?
- What will that look like?

"Reflecting and listening to colleagues' reflections is probably the single most powerful way a teacher improves his or her teaching. Using Data Teams encourages teachers to develop consistency with each other, but does not—and should not—rob them of the creativity they bring to their classrooms.

"One of the secret gifts of participating in the Data Teams process is that it puts you, the teacher, in the exact position you put your students in all the time. It's a learning process, and just when you think you've got all your prior knowledge lined up and you're done, there's something new to learn, think about, and improve upon. I can remember when just assembling the data seemed like an insurmountable task. Now, that's the easy part!"

Here are the insights of Frank Costanzo, Assistant Principal, into Co-Op's Data Teams process: "I began serving as Co-Op's assistant principal during the 2009–2010 school year. I entered an already high-functioning organization with a well-established, coherent Data Teams framework. Because of this, my primary role has become considering the organization's broader scope of work at various levels. This includes refining how we look at data, discerning what the data is explaining, and allowing it to inform our theories and action plans for future practice and analysis.

"As we proceed, I am learning that data is only meaningful if we can discern what it really tells us about what teachers and students do around content. Instructional leadership at Co-Op requires that we stay in close proximity to the work teachers do in their classrooms. You cannot improve problems of practice at the teacher, department, or even building level unless you understand the intricacies of the instructional core from which they derive. Each new set of data results indicators cannot be looked at in isolation, because they build upon previous instructional conditions and decisions."

The Keys to Our Success

Here are some key points about successful implementation of the Data Teams process that we have learned during implementation of the process at Co-Op:

- Support from the district level is critical.
- Ongoing and differentiated professional development is a key element of the process.
- A school culture that supports collaboration in student achievement should be created and fostered.
- Teacher leadership teams must be established.
- A school schedule that supports common planning for teachers should be part of the structure of a building devoted to Data Teams' success.

- Consistent modeling and monitoring of the Data Teams process empowers educators.

- Hiring teachers and administrators who support the Data Teams process is an essential best practice.

Becoming involved in the process of implementing Data Teams requires collaboration, commitment, patience, and a vision of student success. This is truly a *team* effort.

WRITING MY SUCCESS STORY

As you reflect on Co-Op High School's success, think about how their story applies to you in your current setting, and then answer the following questions:

1. The author highlights the importance of careful planning and implementation, as evidenced through the following statement: *"I had to see and approach this endeavor as a* process, *and develop an implementation plan that slowly built internal leadership capacity, starting with the school administrators and lead teachers."*

   What did Co-Op High School do to set the stage, implement, and monitor the Data Teams initiative?

   _____

   _____

   _____

   _____

   _____

2. *"In order to bring this process to the teachers at Co-Op, it had to be embedded in the culture of the school."*

   What does the author mean by this statement? What practices, processes, and beliefs are currently embedded in the culture of your school?

   _____

   _____

   _____

   _____

   _____

3. Co-Op High School uses questions like those below to guide their Data Team meetings. Do your collaborative team meetings incorporate a deliberate structure such as this? Why do you think using such a method leads to improved student achievement and empowered educators?

- What are the students doing well?

- What are the students *not* doing well?

- What is the *specific* plan to address the area(s) in which the students are not doing well? In addition, what is the *specific* plan to address the needs of the students who are already proficient?

- What is the evidence that the strategy is being taught (adult actions)?

- What is the evidence that the strategy is working (student outcomes)?

- What is the date by which the effectiveness of the strategy will be assessed?

_____

_____

_____

_____

_____

4. At the end of the chapter, the author reminds her readers of essential considerations and best practices for anyone who wants to implement Data Teams at the school, district, or central office level. Which of the seven elements of successful implementation resonate with you? Explain.

_____

_____

_____

_____

_____

SUCCESS STORY TWO

Landmark Elementary School, Watsonville, California

"Designing our own rubrics and developing our own strategies to improve student writing made us feel like we were breaking the rules. Instruction became focused on student needs and grade-level standards, instead of a single program or assessment. Data Teams empowered us to do what was best for our students, not just what a program told us to do."

—Jennie Chae, Kindergarten Teacher

SUCCESSFUL CLIENT:	Landmark Elementary School
LOCATION:	Watsonville, California (South of Santa Cruz, suburban)
POPULATION:	600 students K–5 (62 percent English Language Learners)
AUTHOR:	Jennifer Wildman, Principal

It is no coincidence that we are called the Landmark Dragonflies. Our school has gone through—and continues to go through—a metamorphosis. It hasn't always been an easy flight, but we've depended on each other to ride together throughout our journey. As a staff, we have always supported collaboration and implemented the curriculum to the best of our abilities. The use of Data Teams helped to give us focus, and has enabled us to be more successful than we ever dreamed possible. The journey has been long and hard, but has been well worth the effort. So spread your wings and get ready to learn how our school has learned not just to fly, but to soar.

About Landmark Elementary School

One would think that visitors to Landmark Elementary School would comment on its beautiful setting, right next to the wetlands with a distant view of the ocean on a clear day, but the first thing most people notice is our friendly staff, our happy students, and the overall feeling that Landmark is a special place. The best part of our school is the people in our school community.

Our school is six years "new" in the Pajaro Valley Unified School District, south of Santa Cruz, in Watsonville, California. We have about 600 K–5 students, 89 percent of whom are Hispanic and 84 percent of whom are eligible for free or reduced lunches (low socio-economic status). Sixty-two percent of our students are English Language Learners. While most of our students speak Spanish, we also have students who speak Tagalog, Filipino, Mixteco, and other languages. Only 28 percent of our students' parents report graduating from high school. We have some special programs, including a deaf and hard-of-hearing special class, for the 10 percent of our students who have disabilities. Ten percent of our students are in the Gifted and Talented Education program, and 21 percent are considered migrant.

While our school is relatively new, our staff is not. Seven years ago, most of our current staff members worked at another school in the district that was about to close. In response, our staff went to the school board and the board granted our wish to stay together. Every staff member was invited to join the faculty of a new school that would open in the fall. The principal, custodian, cafeteria manager, instructional aides, special education teachers, office staff, and classroom teachers all came to open Landmark School the following August.

Opening a new school presented many challenges: students were combined from seven different district elementary schools, construction delays and building problems continued throughout the year, and we were charged with establishing our school community from the ground up. Some of the students knew each other; however, the new site and the new staff members were unfamiliar to everyone. We

FIGURE 2.1

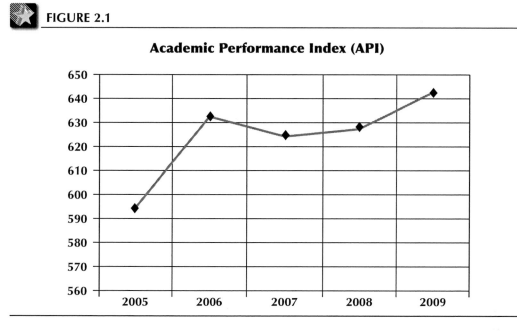

Academic Performance Index (API)

worked tirelessly to set up rules, routines, and expectations, as well as to build relationships with our students and their families. Influenced by our ongoing efforts to create an expectation of collaboration and academic success for all, students, parents, and teachers began to come together as a school community. As a result of our hard work, student achievement levels increased considerably from the first year to the second year of operation. Our overall results, however, remained

FIGURE 2.2

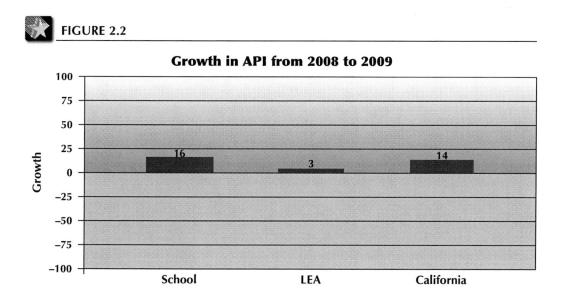

Growth in API from 2008 to 2009

low enough that we entered Program Improvement under the No Child Left Behind Act during our third year, in the fall of 2006. The entire school district entered Program Improvement at that time.

Figure 2.1 shows our school's Academic Performance Index (API), which is a state measure of overall academic growth over time. Note the drop between 2006 and 2007, and the continual rise since then. From 2008 to 2009, our API went up sixteen points, more than both district and state average growth (Figure 2.2).

Before Data Teams—The Cotton Candy Wall

In 2006, our school leadership changed. Formerly an assistant principal and reading coach, I became the principal, and Roberto Torres, who was formerly a classroom teacher, became the assistant principal. Our first year was filled with the usual challenges new administrators face, as well as some significant tragedies that affected our entire school community. Every time we recovered from one event, another unfortunate incident would occur. As we tried to recover from these tragedies, we were informed we would receive a High Priority Schools Grant, which would provide a significant amount of funding for our school in the coming years. As part of the grant qualifications, we had to develop a specific plan to improve student achievement.

Our planning team convened, and we spent several days looking at data as evidence of our current state of teaching and learning. We went on numerous classroom walk-throughs in our own school and made visits to several other neighboring sites. We spent hours trying to determine what obstacles stood between our current state and our desired state—becoming a high-achieving school. We studied the work of effective schools by reading professional books about leadership and school change. Learning about the successful practices of the 90/90/90 schools (schools with at least 90 percent of students in poverty, at least 90 percent minority students, and at least 90 percent of students achieving state standards), where nearly every student was proficient, convinced us that if those schools with similar demographics and challenges could raise their students' scores and empower students and teachers, then we could do it, too.

From my experience with the California Reading and Literature Project, it was always my dream to work in a school that embraced the principles of in-depth data analysis, teacher leadership, and collaboration. Roberto and I asked our staff to imagine a school where teachers were true leaders and everyone worked cohesively. We asked them to help us make our vision of a deeply collaborative teaching environment a reality. After we read *Results Now* (2006) by Michael Schmoker, I invited him to speak to our staff. He agreed, and when he spoke, he hit a nerve.

While we were a positive group of educators and worked really hard, we had not been able to obtain the achievement results we wanted. Mr. Schmoker introduced us to the Data Teams process, which helped us realize that we needed to make some important changes to how we approached teaching and learning. He then encouraged us to consider a long-term commitment to work with The Leadership and Learning Center.

One of our literacy coaches, Lor Larsen, said, "It is like we keep coming up against a 'cotton candy wall.' We had the best intentions and we wanted to make a difference, but every time we made a little headway, we just bounced back to the way we had always been; experiencing the same results we'd always gotten." We knew that to break through the wall, we needed to take swift and decisive actions to improve our school.

When the planning team met for the last time to finalize our High Priority Schools Grant plan, we looked critically at the ideas we had brainstormed, and noticed that they looked remarkably similar to the program we already had in place. At that time, Roberto and I put forth a proposal to work with The Leadership and Learning Center. Our brave planning team made a leap of faith in deciding to work with The Center to develop practices that would help our students achieve; most notably the implementation of Data Teams. We were determined to make the dramatic changes necessary to help our students achieve beyond what we had hoped for.

"Did life exist before Data Teams?" one of teachers joked at a recent meeting. For years we had worked together in grade-level teams and used data to set goals, but effective grade-level communication and shared strategies really did not exist. We used to spend meeting time debating about what percentage of our students could and should meet their goals, and then tried to plan activities that would help us meet those goals.

We bargained for how many students we wanted to reach proficiency. For example, we said, "Shouldn't we set the goal at 100 percent if we expect all students to achieve?" and then "Isn't that too high? We'll never make it. How about 85 percent?" We almost never met the goals we set, and when we failed, we would abandon the old goals in favor of new ones we thought we might actually be able to meet. Even when we were successful, we set off in a new direction, unable to replicate our success in successive data cycles. We knew we were missing a key ingredient: a predictable and reliable structure for setting and meeting achievable goals for student learning.

When we began working with Laura Besser, our consultant from The Leadership and Learning Center, the first thing we learned we needed to do was focus. Our school and district had many initiatives, but we needed to concentrate on just a few goals and strategies that would make the biggest difference. This continues to be the greatest lesson we learn during each and every data cycle. Working with Laura, and reading Dr. Douglas Reeves' book *The Daily Disciplines of Leadership* (2002), convinced us we needed to take a closer look at our students' writing. It was evident that writing was an area worthy of our focus, and one that would have a big impact on all areas of student learning.

By looking at both cause and effect data, we learned that our students' writing was poor because our instruction was inconsistent. Writing instruction had been based on different programs over the years and did not focus enough on the process of writing. The rubrics we were using were not friendly to students or teachers, nor were they being used effectively to evaluate and improve student writing. The writing program offered by our state-adopted core language arts program didn't even introduce writing instruction until the middle of first grade. Most teachers taught only what was going to be assessed and no more. When we walked through classrooms looking for evidence of student writing, we found very little current writing, and what we did find was of questionable quality. Even worse, both teachers and students were "writing-avoidant." Our haphazard writing instruction had to change.

Year One Implementation—Beginning to Believe

At our first meeting the following year, each teacher received a glittery star wand that said "Believe," to represent our belief that every student could succeed in reaching high academic goals, and belief in ourselves that we could make it happen. Our first attempts at improving writing instruction, however, were not necessarily sparkling. The teachers agreed to start every day with writing instruction and student writing time. At first, we wondered what to do during that time; we were unsure how we would fill the thirty minutes. We constructed the instruction plan together. Our meeting time was used to evaluate student writing together and determine our students' strengths and weaknesses. These meetings were long and intense. Our teachers were accustomed to being guided by curriculum that told them what to teach; now they were being asked to use their expertise to make decisions and take action to improve student writing.

"Designing our own rubrics and developing our own strategies to improve student writing made us feel like we were breaking the rules. Instruction became focused on student needs and grade-level standards, instead of a single program or assessment. Data teams empowered us to do what was best for our students, not just what a program told us to do," said kindergarten teacher Jennie Chae.

The curriculum became a resource instead of a rule book. Teachers were given permission to make collaborative instructional decisions that would help their students make progress.

Over the first few weeks, grade levels worked together to narrow both the district goal of academic achievement and our school goal of improving language arts achievement with a laser-like focus on improving writing organization. Teams selected grade-level standards and began the Data Teams process.

Although it would be nice to say the transition was a smooth ride, in reality it was anything but easy. We changed our leadership structure to include Data Team leaders and junior Data Team leaders, and assigned every staff member to a team. We met with the team leaders for a full day of training, and then monthly, to make sure they understood how to support their teams through the process. For the first six months of the year, the entire staff met weekly for two hours to painstakingly go through the steps of analyzing student writing, determining strengths and weaknesses, setting goals, planning instructional strategies, and determining results indicators. We designed teacher and student rubrics based on the grade-level writing standard, and then developed a pre- and post-assessment. When we got the results, we took a moment to celebrate, and then we would start the process all over again. Each step of the way, Roberto and I modeled and then monitored the Data Teams process while the staff worked. We would highlight one step of the Data Teams process in front of the group, and then the teachers would do that step with their team. Then, we'd go to the next step. Our first Data Team meeting took eight hours—a month of weekly two-hour meetings! Every meeting included guided written reflections and time for teams to share struggles and successes with the whole staff.

Monitoring the Data Teams process was only part of the work we did to ensure our success. Roberto and I attended numerous trainings about Data-Driven Decision Making, Data Teams, and Power Standards with The Leadership and Learning Center. We also attended the Leaders in Transition Institute in Boston. The support that Laura Besser (our consultant from The Center) gave us during site visits was essential. She met with our Data Teams, addressed professional development needs, and supported our team leaders. She helped Roberto and I reflect on what we were doing, and where we were headed. She was responsive, and tailored her support to our needs.

Over the course of the school year, we spent hours going over the Data Teams process; reading teacher reflections, designing meeting strategies, and refining our approach to supporting our Data Teams. Analyzing the strengths and obstacles of each team helped us plan professional development activities to improve our results. We faced each obstacle head-on, helping teachers continually raise expectations, narrow their focus, and develop and refine instructional strategies. At first, teachers grappled with frustration at changing course in their instruction, and we struggled with how to support them. In the end, intense collaboration has brought our staff closer together, but at the beginning it was a challenge to work so closely together. Through it all, Laura kept reassuring us that it was all part of the process.

Looking back, a common struggle our teachers, Roberto, and I experienced was "letting go" of the way we operated in the past. We had to get rid of structures and processes that didn't work. We had to set aside our preconceived notions and ideas of how our school *should* be, and had to jump into the ongoing process of creating the school we knew we *could* be. Because of the Data Teams process, we learned new roles, took on new responsibilities, and became highly accountable to each other and to our students. Collectively, we allowed ourselves to make as many mistakes as it took to get things right during the Data Teams process. When we were distracted, we helped each other to refocus. When we needed to change course, we encouraged each other to make the changes that needed to be made in order for us to achieve our goals.

By the end of the year, we were all exhausted, but we had nearly 70 percent of our students writing proficiently at their grade-level standard. Our end-of-year Data Teams celebration was held with a "Gilligan's Island" theme, where teams made a presentation to the staff about their trip through the year.

While it helped to have the funding from the High Priority Schools Grant to make these changes, including the ability to pay teachers for their overtime collaboration, the work was intense and difficult. The reward, however, was empowering ourselves to change our school. "It felt like we had regained our professionalism," said third-grade teacher Cynthia Torres. We had survived a year of intensive change and were able to celebrate our success.

Year Two—Refining Our Implementation and Expanding Our Vision

After having implemented Data Teams over an entire school year, we felt confident we would have an easier second year. In some ways, this was true. The teachers felt that being more familiar with the Data Teams process would free up energy to focus even more on student learning. But for administrators, things got a little harder. While teams operated more independently, we struggled with finding ways to support teachers in digging deeper into analyzing and using student data to make decisions. We worked harder than ever to keep teams functioning and focused. Setting expectations for timelines, reinforcing routines, and monitoring processes and results became even more important during this time.

At our first meeting, teachers received giant sunglasses, representing our "big vision." Roberto and I worked on helping our teachers revise and articulate the vision that we had for our school and our students. Teachers took more ownership of the Data Teams process, and were more self-directed.

"We had a narrower focus area, but a wider awareness of student abilities, gaps, needs, and successes," said fifth-grade teacher Tomas Rodriguez. "Teams took more risks and built their capacity to respond to student needs. There was a lot less frustration and more flexibility than the previous year. The process became more refined, and teams were able to take on the additional challenge of combining a reading and writing standard into the same data cycles."

As administrators, we were able to tailor professional development to specific team needs. For example, when the fifth-grade team began writing summaries of non-fiction text, we invited a trainer from the Santa Cruz County Office of Education to come teach them about Cornell note-taking. When second-grade teachers wanted to improve their students' ability to use transition words, another county office trainer came to introduce *Step Up to Writing* strategies. We also worked with Susana Dutro from E. L. Achieve to infuse effective English language development strategies into fourth-grade writing instruction for English Language Learners. Each time a team expressed a specific need, Roberto and I tried to help them find resources to meet that need.

Throughout the year, we continued to meet with Data Team leaders on a monthly basis. Because most of the new Data Team leaders had been junior Data Team leaders the previous year, they were more experienced and ready to take things to a new level. One thing we discovered together is the need to continually seek new instructional strategies. It is not surprising that any group of teachers would continue to use the strategies with which they are most familiar. We learned the importance of matching the strategies we chose to the obstacles students faced in their learning. In order to develop new strategies, we had to seek new resources and look outside of our school for research on effective instructional strategies. We sought high-yield instructional strategies from research and professional reading.

As part of our desire to develop a true system of distributed leadership, we created focus groups: vertical teams of teachers studying various areas of the curriculum. The groups, which were led by an instructional coach, read current research in that curricular area, learned new strategies, and shared them with the whole staff. Each Data Team had at least one teacher in each focus group, which meant sharing could happen informally during Data Team meetings. Focus group members also presented their research topics to the whole staff.

 FIGURE 2.3

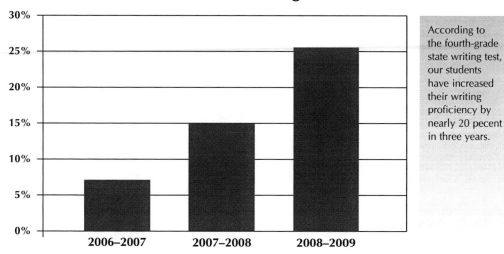

Fourth-Grade State Writing Test Results

According to the fourth-grade state writing test, our students have increased their writing proficiency by nearly 20 pecent in three years.

During the course of the year, we learned again and again about focus. Narrowing our focus actually resulted in a *wider* impact on student reading and writing skills. When expository writing improved, reading scores improved. When students could write a response to literature, their summary writing was better. One teacher compared the process of narrowing their focus to fertilizing a plant at the roots. If you focus on just the right spot, the fertilizer spreads itself around the roots and the plant will thrive.

As a result of our hard work, we saw a marked increase in student achievement on our state English language arts test, particularly among students who had been at our school for the entire two-year period that we had been using data cycles. While we still had a long way to go until we would be satisfied with our overall levels of student achievement, we knew we were headed in the right direction.

Figure 2.3 shows our fourth-grade state writing test results over the last three years.

Figure 2.4 shows our California state test results in English language arts. We began implementing Data Teams in 2007, and the percentage of proficient students in English language arts has increased by more than 7 percent since that time.

At the end of the year, the team leaders asked me if they could design the Data Teams celebration. Whereas last year we had celebrated with an island party, this year the teachers wanted to "pass the torch" to the next grade level in a vertical team activity. Each team created a display board and a binder containing Data Team records, student writing samples, rubrics, teacher reflections, and results to describe

 **FIGURE 2.4**

English Language Arts Trend Analysis Graph

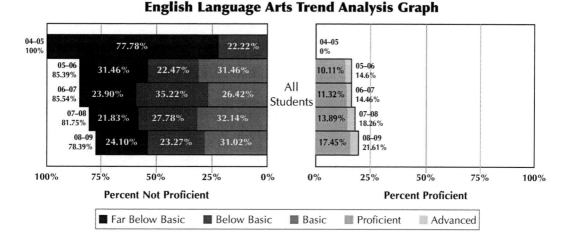

what students had learned throughout the year. With little more than one week of school to go, the teachers developed an intense and focused activity much more challenging than anything Roberto and I would ever have dreamed of asking them to do at that time of year. During the activity, teams of teachers traveled from table to table, visiting neighboring grade level teams to learn about their Data Team stories. Passing the torch to the next grade level meant that new teams would be able to start students at a higher level right at the beginning of the next school year. Because the end-of-the-year Data Teams celebration was created by and meaningful to the teachers, the depth of dialogue and articulation between teams was unprecedented.

Year Three—Embracing the Journey

At the end of the previous school year, we nearly lost several classroom teaching positions to budget cuts at the state and district levels. With luck and creativity, we were able to retain all of our classroom teachers, but we experienced dramatically decreased levels of support staff in all other departments, including academic coaches, library staff, custodial and cafeteria services, and health and office staff. This created stress on many levels. As site administrators, we were distracted from our focus on curriculum and instruction; we were tied up finding solutions for the day-to-day operation problems of the school. Fortunately, our school district began to implement Data Teams and Power Standards across the board.

As we began the year, teachers received a shiny river rock to represent the journey ahead. River rocks are both shaped by the river and make the river take shape. We knew it would take all of us to embrace the journey and make the year successful. During this difficult time, our confident and competent teams of teachers began their Data Teams with decreased direction. They began collecting and analyzing student data, setting goals, teaching, and planning collaboratively on their own. When the school systems were again in order, Roberto and I were able to rejoin the Data Teams in progress.

In addition to the way we've implemented Data Teams in the past, this year we've added data cycles in other academic areas based on Power Standards that we "unwrapped" together. We have learned more about creating Big Ideas and Essential Questions to match our Power Standards. We have studied higher-order thinking skills, and helped infuse them into our instruction. Carefully choosing Power Standards has allowed us to optimize student learning based on long-term goals. We've focused on these Power Standards in order to address skills and concepts that will help students progress through the curriculum, advance to ever-increasing academic levels, and apply what they've learned to their entire lives. Power Standards have helped ensure that instruction in all academic areas is more meaningful and engaging.

One of the teachers wrote, "Now, I think: 'Will this lesson be meaningful in their lives?'—not just 'Will it fulfill a mandate or requirement?' and not just 'Will it be fun?,' but 'Can it transfer into a usable skill? Will it create more learning?'" We've let go of our dependence on pacing calendars and started backward mapping to reach our goals by the end of each school year. Teachers work together to determine the most powerful strategies, which has resulted in an increase in rigor for student learning. Most importantly, we've developed the expectation that *all* students will be proficient in the Power Standards we've selected.

We've made lots of mistakes along the way, but implementing Data Teams and Power Standards has changed the fundamental way we go about the business of teaching and learning at our school. We've learned what works, and, even more importantly, what *doesn't* work, and what detracts from instruction. Teachers spend less time compiling data and more time analyzing it. Collaborative decision making is valued at our school above all else.

One teacher commented about Data Teams with the reflection, "It feels ingrained in how I think about everything I do…I focus on what the data says first, then on what I can do to help students learn." We've improved our ability to let the kids tell us where they are academically and to respond to that information in our instruction. We've also increased the role students play in goal-setting and evaluating what they've learned.

As administrators, we've learned to trust our teachers to collaboratively plan targeted and intentional instruction, and discovered that teachers need to be given permission and support to make decisions and take action. We've also learned how to help our teams become more effective by combining teachers that work well together, providing resources, planning immediate and relative professional development, and reflecting on and monitoring teamwork and instruction. Ultimately, our internal results show that we are achieving continual growth.

First-grade teacher Darci Cristobal said, "The most inspiring part of Data Teams is that it allows us, as teachers, to do what we do best: use our creativity, our skills, and, best of all, our instinct in knowing what's best for our students. Wasn't this our goal when we became teachers in the first place?"

One thing that has become apparent to us is that Data Teams result in continually increasing expectations. Students often meet long-term goals much earlier than expected, so then we are able to develop even more rigorous goals. Data Teams also result in differentiation; we identify students by name, analyze their strengths and obstacles, and target instructional strategies to meet their specific needs.

Our writing results over the 2008–2009 school year show the waves of changes teachers are able to make as students meet goals and new ones are set.

FIGURE 2.5

	Cycle One		Cycle Two		Cycle Three		Cycle Four		Cycle Five	
	PRE	POST	PRE	POST	PRE	POST	PRE	POST	PRE	POST
K	48%	79%	16%	37%	9%	84%	27%	95%	40%	75%
1	30%	79%	8%	75%	6%	53%	53%	59%	7%	72%
2	9%	58%	45%	56%	21%	45%	45%	42%	42%	63%
3	27%	48%	22%	56%	12%	65%	65%	55%	23%	56%
4	19%	25%	29%	61%	31%	30%	31%	18%	31%	83%
5	56%	65%	65%	83%	8%	45%	3%	20%	20%	55%
	31%	59%	31%	61%	15%	54%	37%	48%	27%	67%
LANDMARK DATA TEAMS 2009										

Figure 2.5 shows our Data Team results during the 2008–2009 school year. An example of our increasingly higher standards can be seen on the chart in first grade: when the percentage of students proficient is high for a post-test (in cycle two), a lower pretest score in the next column (cycle three) indicates the setting of a new and more rigorous goal for the next data cycle.

Sustaining Data Teams—The Unstoppable Force

Implementing Data Teams has improved our students' achievement, particularly in writing, our original area of focus. Our expectations for student learning continually increase. One of our teachers said, "The students could do so much more than we thought they could." When asked, many of our students say writing is their favorite subject. The amount of time students spend writing each day is increasing. We are learning to incorporate writing into every academic subject, and students are able to write about those subjects with increasing levels of organization and focus. Their use of vocabulary has expanded dramatically. They are learning to edit, revise, and evaluate their own and their peers' writing. Most astonishing, although it is not an area on which we have focused, our students' writing shows an incredible use of voice. The idea that writing is, as author Stephen King says, "thinking from the end of a pen," (a favorite quote of Dr. Reeves) is a reality for our students now.

We have noticed several unexpected results from implementing Data Teams beyond improved student writing. Writing has become the way our students express themselves, request things, and tell their stories. They are able to participate and contribute to our school with their writing. Our school climate, already very positive, has soared. Visitors always tell us that our students and staff seem very happy. We have noticed a decrease in student discipline issues, and an increase in students' ability to solve problems. Staff turnover is near zero. We haven't hired a new classroom teacher since our first year of implementing Data Teams, three years ago.

As a principal, I think it is very important to broaden our perspectives beyond just what we've learned in our own site implementation. Our staff has worked collaboratively with the teachers of many neighboring elementary schools over the last three years. This work helped influence the decision of our district to begin working with The Leadership and Learning Center to implement Data Teams and Power Standards K–12. To support this implementation, teams of Landmark teachers traveled to two of our feeder high schools to participate in a panel discussion, which helped inform and motivate teachers to implement Data Teams. We have helped support district administrators and teachers during their early trainings and implementation sessions. We've also worked with school teams outside of our district and county, at least one of which has now begun working with The Center to develop Data Teams at their site. We will continue to seek opportunities to share what we've learned and to learn from others. It is all part of our ongoing desire to improve our school.

At Landmark, we will continue to respond to our students' needs by expanding Data Teams into all academic areas. We would like to learn more about formative assessments. We are working on ways to integrate Data Teams and Power Standards with the principles of Response to Intervention. Merging the processes we have learned into one seamless approach to instruction and student learning will be a challenge, but it is one that we are well-equipped to handle. After implementing Data Teams, we know we can do anything!

Our staff can say with confidence that Data Teams will be an integral part of Landmark School forever. How do we know? We believe that what we do makes a difference, and we are committed to continuing to grow and learn together. Aside from my reflections as the principal, this Data Teams success story was collaboratively written by the teachers of Landmark School. This is not *my* story; it is *our* story.

Our entire school community works together to support student learning, including our support staff members in all departments. We are grateful to them and to the teachers who work tirelessly to ensure our students learn more and more each day: Carolyn Ames, Ellie Aucoin-Unruhe, Veronica Barrios, Kim Black, Jennie Chae, Darci Cristobal, Ethan Cristobal, Corinne Evans, Cindy Galos, Crystal Geiger, Elida Guerrero, Roisin Gunn, Holly Hatch, Stephanie Hedgpeth-Lopez, Julie Hitchcock, Susan Logue, Lor Larsen, Ann May, Eileen Maxinoski, Anabel Mendez, Christiane Muratet, Lynda Pate, Julie Pierce, Sylvia Qualls, Gerry Rieger, Tomas Rodriguez, Marcia Rothwell, Edith Ruiz, Cynthia Torres, Elena Urbina, Vicki Ward, and Darlene Wilcox. We would also like to express our gratitude for the endless support of administrators Michael Berman and Roberto Torres, who help make things happen at Landmark School.

WRITING MY SUCCESS STORY

As you reflect on Landmark Elementary School's success, take time to think about how their story applies to you in your current setting, and then answer the following questions:

1. One of Landmark Elementary School's literacy coaches is quoted as saying, *"It is like we keep coming up against a 'cotton candy wall.' We had the best intentions and we wanted to make a difference, but every time we made a little headway, we just bounced back to the way we had always been; experiencing the same results we'd always gotten."*

   Have you ever felt this way as an educator, team member, or leader? Explain.

   _____

   _____

   _____

   _____

   _____

2. *"For years we had worked together in grade-level teams and used data to set goals, but effective grade-level communication and shared strategies really did not exist."*

   Have you ever been part of a team that didn't operate to its full potential? In contrast, have you contributed to a high-functioning team? What is the difference between the two experiences?

   _____

   _____

   _____

   _____

   _____

3. *"At our first meeting the following year, each teacher received a glittery star wand that said 'Believe,' to represent our belief that every student could succeed in reaching high academic goals, and belief in ourselves that we could make it happen."*

> This approach, called the "Pygmalion effect" at The Leadership and Learning Center, is essentially the *My Fair Lady* way of viewing teaching and learning—if you look like a lady, and act like a lady, then you're a lady. The research suggests that, as self-help author Wayne Dyer says, "When you change the way you look at things, the things you look at change."

> How do currently see the educators you work with, and the students you influence?

_____

_____

_____

_____

_____

4. *"Looking back, a common struggle our teachers, Roberto, and I experienced was 'letting go' of the way we operated in the past. We had to get rid of structures and processes that didn't work. We had to set aside our preconceived notions and ideas of how our school* should *be, and had to jump into the ongoing process of creating the school we knew we* could *be."*

> What can you stop doing, and what can you do more of at your current site, in order to experience greater success?

_____

_____

_____

_____

_____

Lake Villa School District 41, Lake Villa, Illinois

"The formation of learning teams (aka Data Teams) is the most fundamental and essential professional development initiative the district has ever undertaken. This leadership and organizational initiative focuses on greater accountability for achievement results, cultivates a higher degree of staff ownership, and significantly impacts how staff members view their roles in the teaching and learning process."

—John Van Pelt, Superintendent

SUCCESSFUL CLIENT:	Lake Villa School District 41
LOCATION:	Lake Villa, Illinois (Northeast corner of Illinois, suburban)
POPULATION:	3,300 students
AUTHOR:	John Van Pelt, Ed.D., Superintendent

Background

Lake Villa School District 41 is a suburban school district of 3,300 students located in the northeast corner of Illinois, approximately 60 miles from Chicago. Our district has one PreK–6 elementary school, three K–6 elementary schools, and one grades 7–8 middle school. Although the school district is comprised primarily of non-minority, middle-income households, racial and socio-economic demographics are becoming increasingly diverse. We have maintained strong community and parent support in our district. During the 2005–2006 school year, District 41 was in the process hiring a new superintendent.

The Board of Education, community, and staff identified essential characteristics for the new superintendent as part of the search process. The characteristics included: creating and maintaining a coordinated and articulated district-wide curriculum; developing strong working relationships with staff; motivating staff to strive for excellence; managing the district's financial and human resources; creating and monitoring a strategic plan and vision for the school district; setting long-range and short-range goals; and communicating with staff, students, community, and the Board of Education. I was hired as the new superintendent, and I began my duties on July 1, 2006.

On October 18, 2006, I convened the Lake Villa District 41 Comprehensive Accountability Task Force, which consisted of a diverse group of school-level administrators, central office administrators, parents and guardians, and community members. Throughout the 2006–2007 school year, the task force was immersed in the Comprehensive Accountability Plan philosophy and structure derived from the book *Accountability in Action: A Blueprint for Learning Organizations* (2000) by Douglas B. Reeves. The task force met monthly over a period of seven months to form recommendations to guide District 41.

The central mission of the task force was to create a Comprehensive Accountability Plan that would seamlessly align the district's accountability indicators. The plan analyzes relevant data and provides pertinent information regarding district initiatives, including initiatives having the greatest impact on District 41 schools. This information is communicated through a "District Dashboard" to staff, students, the community, and the Board of Education three times each school year. The Comprehensive Accountability Plan also provides a basis and support for individual School Improvement Plans.

Prior to the development of the Comprehensive Accountability Plan, each school in the district had different goals and professional development plans, as well as inconsistent School Improvement Plans. Professional development opportunities varied widely from school to school. Staff members needed the knowledge and experience to develop Common Formative Assessments, analyze data to make informed decisions, develop appropriate and effective instructional strategies, and plan timely interventions when students did not make satisfactory progress.

At the district level, the curriculum was only loosely aligned with the Illinois Learning Standards, and few teachers utilized curriculum documents. There were significant variations in curriculum content and curriculum delivery across the district. The district did not have a strategic plan, a common vision, or any long-range or short-range improvement goals. There were no accountability measures in place other than those required by the state. Finally, there was only a loosely organized evaluation system for teachers, and there was no evaluation system for administrators.

As a result of our work on the Comprehensive Accountability Plan, Lake Villa teachers now have curricula and assessments aligned to state standards, professional development aligned with the district's long-term goals, and clearly articulated goals and expectations aligned to the Comprehensive Accountability Plan for each school. All administrators are evaluated annually on individual goals, which are aligned with school goals and district goals. Furthermore, the district has made tremendous strides in student achievement between 2006 and 2009.

Why Data Teams?

In Lake Villa School District 41, we refer to Data Teams as "learning teams." The formation of learning teams is the most fundamental and essential professional development initiative the district has ever undertaken. This leadership and organizational initiative focuses on greater accountability for achievement results, cultivates a higher degree of staff ownership, and significantly impacts how staff members view their roles in the teaching and learning process. Teacher collaboration, with a clearly defined focus and purpose, has become a powerful tool to increase learning and achievement.

In the Data Teams process, teachers collaborate in small grade-level and/or subject-area learning teams to develop short-range and long-range goals to improve student achievement based on data analysis. Our learning teams meet weekly and have established roles and responsibilities to facilitate ongoing analysis. The process includes an analysis of strengths and obstacles, development of specific instructional strategies to support improvement, development of common assessments, selection of indicators so team members know when progress is being made, and interventions when students are not making satisfactory progress. Ongoing professional development is provided to staff so that appropriate modifications in classroom instruction can be made.

The instruction of students and its impact, based on results, is the purpose of team collaboration, planning, and monitoring. The Comprehensive Accountability Plan, which provides direction for continuous monitoring and reporting of improvement over time, is put into action across the district primarily through the work of the district's forty learning teams (Data Teams). Any school district accountability plan, strategic plan, or School Improvement Plan has very limited effectiveness until it impacts learning at a classroom level and student level.

Curriculum development in our district is essentially a three-step process. The first step is the formation of a district curriculum committee. The core curriculum areas of literacy (reading, writing, speaking, listening), math, social studies, and science include representatives from every building and grade level. Curriculum committees, chaired by the assistant superintendent of teaching and learning, develop the curriculum framework or design. Curriculum committees also evaluate the current curriculum during this phase. Second, student outcomes, aligned to Illinois state standards and college readiness standards, are identified for every grade level. Additionally, district-wide Common Formative Assessments are developed so that learning teams can monitor student progress. Instructional materials, adopted by the Board of Education to support the curriculum, are purchased by the district. Finally, the district provides district-wide professional development and support for implementation of the curriculum. The first year of implementation is closely monitored by the central office, building administrators, and staff, so that adjustments can be made when needed. The primary focus for the district is literacy.

In order to support the new curricula and Comprehensive Accountability Plan, district-wide professional development was provided as the foundation for the work of the learning teams and district staff. Our professional development included:

- Data Teams and Data-Driven Decision Making (now titled Decision Making for Results)
- Classroom walk-through observations with reflective conversations
- Making Standards Work (now titled Engaging Classroom Assessments)
- Common Formative Assessments
- Professional Learning Communities

Beginning August 2006, central office administrators, building administrators, and approximately four teachers per building completed training for the implementation of Professional Learning Communities. The training was based on the book *Professional Learning Communities at Work: Best Practices for Enhancing*

Student Achievement (1998) by Richard DuFour and Robert Eaker. Upon completion, the principals and trained staff facilitated school-based professional development sessions on Professional Learning Communities within their own buildings. In Professional Learning Communities, educators work closely together as a group to ensure the success of all students.

I facilitated walk-through training, based on the book *The Three-Minute Classroom Walk-Through: Changing School Supervisory Practice One Teacher at a Time* (2004) by Carolyn Downey, Fenwick W. English, and Betty Steffy, for administrators in October 2006. Any new administrators are also trained. Administrators conduct walk-through observations, which allow them to monitor the progress of district initiatives and collaboratively reflect with teachers and other administrators.

Data Teams and Data-Driven Decision Making (now called Decision Making for Results) training was conducted for all certified staff. The primary goal of The Leadership and Learning Center's Data Teams seminar was to instruct Lake Villa teachers how to maximize effective instructional practice via constant monitoring of student progress. This seminar gave Lake Villa staff the tools to analyze relevant student data effectively in collaborative teams, and provided structure and substance to our meetings. Teachers applied results not only to inform instruction for individual students, but also to evaluate and improve core general education practices and the overall effectiveness of interventions. The superintendent, assistant superintendent of teaching and learning, and principals meet with learning teams weekly during the school year. Ongoing evaluations of the implementation of the accountability plan are completed and shared three times per year. All administrators are trained in making informal, walk-through classroom observations and conducting follow-up conversations with teachers as part of the monitoring process.

The Leadership and Learning Center's Making Standards Work trainings (now called Engaging Classroom Assessments) provided Lake Villa educators with strategies to create standards-based performance assessments that directly align with Illinois curriculum and priority standards. Approximately fifty teachers, all of whom were involved in the development of the new district reading curriculum, received this training. The assessments designed in this seminar provided an effective means to improve student performance in the classroom and on high-stakes standardized tests, and could measure student achievement results. Participants learned why performance tasks for assessing student proficiency along with accompanying rubrics are so powerful. They also saw compelling research that links writing across the curriculum with higher standardized test scores.

The Leadership and Learning Center's Common Formative Assessments seminar provided Lake Villa educators with training to create interim assessments, collaboratively designed by grade-level or course teams. Assessments are administered to all students in a grade level or course several times during the school year. These Common Formative Assessments are similar in design and format to district and Illinois state assessments, and results can be analyzed and utilized via the processes learned in the Decision Making for Results training. All Lake Villa certified staff received Common Formative Assessments training in October 2007. Common Formative Assessments are now an integral part of the Lake Villa curriculum development process.

What Data Teams Implementation Looks Like at Lake Villa

One of the earliest professional development commitments we made in Lake Villa School District was to maintain two certified Data Teams trainers in the district. I was already a certified trainer. Alex Barbour, Assistant Superintendent of Teaching and Learning, received his certification from The Leadership and Learning Center in 2006. During the 2006–2007 school year, eleven training sessions were conducted for approximately 200 staff members over a period of four months. This proved to be an incredible opportunity for myself and Mr. Barbour to work with Lake Villa staff. Data Teams training is also provided to new staff annually, so all certified staff completes the training. Because the training is done in-house, the district has established a high level of professional expertise and sustainable capacity, and will save money on future professional development costs.

During the 2006–2007 school year, Lake Villa also established team leaders to facilitate and guide the work of learning teams. For teams to function efficiently and effectively, someone on the team must assume a leadership role. In high schools, department chairs perform a similar function. As team leaders, teachers assume leadership roles throughout the district and have more ownership and accountability for student learning and achievement. Learning teams enhance the capacity of the teaching staff to fully implement the district curriculum, monitor student progress through Common Formative Assessments, and implement the work of the Comprehensive Accountability Plan at the building, grade, and classroom level.

Principals have the responsibility to monitor the work of individual teams, conduct brief but regular meetings with each team, and offer resources, support, and assistance where needed.

Team leaders:

• Are selected by colleagues or are appointed by the principal.

• Facilitate learning team meetings.

• Encourage active listening and participation.

• Commit to a one-year term.

• Demonstrate leadership qualities.

• Believe in the learning team process.

Learning teams may be configured somewhat differently in different schools, depending on the structure of each school. In elementary schools, teams are organized by grade level. In the middle school, teams are organized by both subject and grade. Special education, reading resource, and English Language Learner teachers meet regularly with learning teams in their respective schools. Specialty teachers (music, art, technology) have district-wide learning teams. Physical education teachers have teams at both the elementary and middle school levels. Specialty teams coordinate curriculum, develop Common Formative Assessments, assess student progress, and report results on a regular basis. Specialty teams also directly support Lake Villa's focus on literacy by incorporating reading and writing into specialty areas.

All learning teams follow The Leadership and Learning Center's Data Teams process:

• Collect and chart data

• Analyze strengths and obstacles

• Establish (SMART) goals: set, review, revise

- Select instructional strategies (what teachers will do for students)
- Determine results indicators (what students can do so teachers know progress has been made)

The frequency and length of learning team meetings varies from weekly to monthly. Grade-level and subject-area teams in the elementary schools and the middle school meet weekly. Teams may meet from 60 to 100 minutes per week. Teams that meet on a weekly basis have more success improving the achievement levels of students who had not been demonstrating proficiency. Learning teams report results each trimester. Results are communicated through newsletters, Web pages, data walls, and through a "dashboard" reporting system. This provides the staff, students, community, and Board of Education with updates on student performance in a variety of formats.

To coordinate the work of the learning teams throughout the building, each school has a building leadership team. That team consists of the principal, lead teacher/assistant principal, and team leaders. Building leadership teams meet at least monthly to discuss progress on goals, achievement gaps, successes and challenges, progress monitoring, assessment schedules and results, intervention needs, and resources.

One of the greatest benefits of the Data Teams process is collaboration to develop strategies and interventions when students are not meeting expectations. Flexible grouping of students within a grade-level team to address the short-term learning needs of individual students has become a prominent strategy in Lake Villa. Another significant aspect of the learning team process is the district's Response to Intervention. Response to Intervention is aligned with district professional development and the Comprehensive Accountability Plan, and is an integral component of the reading curriculum and the work of learning teams. The three-tier intervention system is incorporated into the entire learning team process, ongoing review of assessment results, and the development of strategies and interventions to help students reach proficiency.

It is difficult to overstate the importance of professional development to the success of learning teams. Well-defined professional development and ongoing support is the key to the success and effectiveness of learning teams. All professional development goals remain aligned with the Lake Villa Comprehensive Accountability Plan. In addition to district-wide professional development to support the curriculum and specific program implementation, the district has instituted two literacy coach positions to provide ongoing professional development for implementation of the reading and writing curriculum and utilization of reading benchmark assessments.

Results of Implementation of Data Teams

Data Teams play a prominent and central role in Lake Villa, and have impacted student learning and achievement. Lake Villa students have made significant gains on the Illinois Standards Achievement Test (ISAT). Between 2006 and 2009, the percentage of students proficient or above in ISAT reading increased from 78.8 to 84.9; ISAT math increased from 88.4 to 90.3 (Figure 3.1). Perhaps most noteworthy has been the progress made in student writing performance. Although not shown in Figure 3.1, the district-wide average for the writing portion of the ISAT has increased from 50 percent proficient to 72 percent proficient. In addition, the district's focus on literacy, with particular emphasis on writing, has helped boost ISAT scores in both reading and science.

The implementation of a Comprehensive Accountability Plan, new writing curriculum, Data Teams, and comprehensive professional development is transforming Lake Villa School District 41. The district is implementing a new reading curriculum during the 2009–2010 school year. Teachers are assuming new roles as leadership is visible across the district, and the capacity of staff to meet learning challenges continues to grow. Staff efficacy is clearly increasing. This

FIGURE 3.1

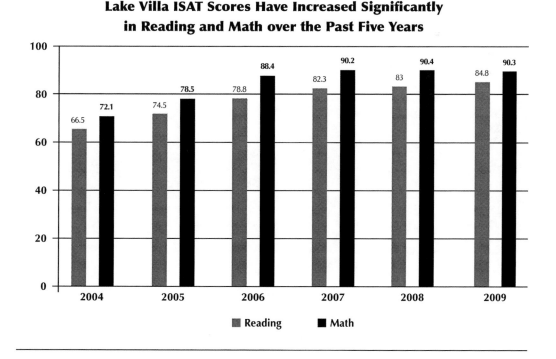

Lake Villa ISAT Scores Have Increased Significantly in Reading and Math over the Past Five Years

transformation represents deep systemic change. In many ways, Lake Villa is a story of a good school district becoming a great school district. To use an analogy from Jim Collins in *Good to Great* (2001), Lake Villa is experiencing "The Flywheel Effect." During the early stages of learning teams, implementation was slow and challenging as staff learned new skills and new ways of collaborating. Once learning results for students were evident, staff became energized and more committed to the learning team process. Staff members could clearly see the benefits for themselves as well. Learning teams now work as a cohesive whole, and gain strength from one another. This momentum continues to this day and builds incrementally each year.

What We Have Learned

A survey was created by Alex Barbour, Assistant Superintendent of Teaching and Learning, and building Principals Sandy Keim and Scott Klene, to obtain feedback about the Data Teams process. Below is a sample of their responses:

How does working as a learning team promote collegiality?

"We have the ability to collaborate on a continual basis. Each staff member should hopefully feel like he or she is part of a whole and can make contributions to the common goal of student learning effectively. As a team, we have grown to rely on each other and ask for advice and/or resources, which, in turn, have made us stronger teachers and professionals. *Every* district should do this, as the effect is not only on teachers; the 'team atmosphere and mentality' also rubs off onto the students, in that their learning environment is a positive one. Success is felt by all."

"When the goals are identified and expressed explicitly, the team is able to work with those goals in mind. When teams have time to discuss, reflect, and identify common concerns, working as a team becomes the underlying thread that holds us together. Respect is a must, and without a professional respect for each other, collegiality is at risk."

Describe an example of how your learning team works in a collegial manner.

"Our team works each week to plan the implementation of the reading curriculum. We share ideas, materials, and eventually reflections of what worked or what did not work. Based on that knowledge, we plan for the next week, and the cycle continues."

"Our learning team works in a collegial manner sharing our professional knowledge with each other. This gives us the ability to work as a team in which everyone is heard. With this input, we have success."

How do your learning team members support each other?

"When we first began the learning team process, there was not much support for each other. We planned together, but then there would be little communication about how lessons went or how we could improve. But (now), we meet regularly and discuss which strategies worked and which did not. Then the team members offer advice and brainstorm strategies to improve the lesson or the assessment goals."

How does working as a learning team promote school improvement and professional growth?

"I see huge gains in my students' success just from getting together with my team and discussing data, strengths, and weaknesses. I see my students from a different viewpoint at times, just from showing my coworkers student work, and getting their input. It also creates a positive atmosphere. I am comfortable going to (my coworkers) for anything, and that makes me want to come to work each day knowing that my team members are supportive of each other."

"We all have a common goal as a staff. We have different goals to guide us in our grade levels, but the ultimate goal of student growth and achievement is very present in most staff member's minds, lessons, and the environment we create for our students. I love hearing about what worked and what didn't work in other grade levels. I enjoy bouncing ideas off of other teams, since they tend to have a different perspective on things. I love our collaborative building. It is our home away from home, and it really feels like a family, making it enjoyable to work each and every day."

Lake Villa has achieved remarkable results, and Data Teams have been the cornerstone of nearly every successful district initiative. We have learned that change is neither easy nor without controversy, and that all professionals need time to develop new skills and practices, to study what is working and what is not working, to use student data systematically, and to make adjustments when needed. Challenges remain as we review current efforts and new initiatives through a lens focused on the district's primary mission: excellence in teaching and learning. We continue building on what works for our students, sharing leadership, learning from our mistakes, and keeping that big picture in sight.

As the district looks to the future, two noteworthy initiatives are planned and will be implemented in the 2010–2011 school year. First, Lake Villa will implement a standards-based report card. This will align the written curriculum, the taught curriculum, progress monitoring, Common Formative Assessment results for individual students, interventions, and student progress reporting into a single cohesive system. Second, the district is planning to adopt Charlotte Danielson's *Enhancing Professional Practice: A Framework for Teaching* (1996) for teacher evaluation. This research-based framework will define and enhance best practices and support continuous professional growth throughout the school district. In Lake Villa, we know teacher effectiveness, staff collaboration, and commitment to a common purpose are the keys to increasing learner outcomes and student achievement.

WRITING MY SUCCESS STORY

As you reflect on Lake Villa School District 41's success, take time to think about how their story applies to you in your current setting, and then answer the following questions:

1. Throughout this story, the author talks about Lake Villa School District's Comprehensive Accountability Plan. Here is one example: *"As a result of our work on the Comprehensive Accountability Plan, Lake Villa teachers now have curricula and assessments aligned to state standards, professional development aligned with the district's long-term goals, and clearly articulated goals and expectations aligned to the Comprehensive Accountability Plan for each school."*

   Are you aware of any efforts in your school or district that are this deliberate and tightly connected?

   _____

   _____

   _____

   _____

   _____

2. *"Lake Villa learning teams report results each trimester. Results are communicated through newsletters, Web pages, data walls, and through a dashboard reporting system."*

   How does your site communicate results at the individual, team, building, and district levels? Do you practice transparency in the way your data is displayed and discussed?

   _____

   _____

   _____

   _____

   _____

3. The author said, *"One of the greatest benefits of the Data Teams process is collaboration to develop strategies and interventions when students are not meeting expectations."*

> Do you collaborate with your colleagues on a regular basis to develop strategies and interventions? What are some practical next steps that you can implement to discourage "silos" (people who do not value teamwork, and who make decisions without group consensus) and to foster the collaborative environment described above?

_____

_____

_____

_____

_____

4. *"We have learned that change is neither easy nor without controversy, and that all professionals need time to develop new skills and practices, to study what is working and what is not working, to use student data systematically, and to make adjustments when needed."*

> Why is it inevitable that with any type of change, controversy, conflict, and difficulty are predictable companions? Are these elements necessary in order to transform the thinking of a person, team, leader, or system? Explain.

_____

_____

_____

_____

_____

SUCCESS STORY FOUR

Edison Middle School, Bakersfield, California

"Although the Data Teams process may seem sterile and scientific, that is not a limitation. Rather, the process is artistically designed to open doors of communication—and we all know how heavy those castle doors can be!"

—Koleen Lorenzana, Language Arts Teacher

SUCCESSFUL CLIENT:	Edison Middle School
LOCATION:	Bakersfield, California (Rural)
POPULATION:	480 students (41 percent English Language Learners)
AUTHOR:	Koleen Lorenzana, Language Arts Teacher

Before joining the educational team of the Edison School District, I taught language arts to junior high students in a nationally distinguished California Blue Ribbon School. The majority of the students at that school scored proficient or advanced on their California Standards Tests (CSTs), and because of their high performance level, it was difficult to differentiate effective from ineffective teaching practices. Thus, acceptable student performance was thought to equal acceptable instructional methodology.

We teachers were the kings and queens of our classrooms, working with our colleagues to create inter-disciplinary, cross-curricular thematic units. The results were impressive on the surface, as each student participated in lessons and activities that incorporated language arts, social science, science, and mathematics. Each unit was built upon a historical unit or event, and core disciplines were integral and relevant. Student achievement was determined, at times somewhat subjectively, throughout each instructional unit via standards-based, teacher-created rubrics and assessments. Our students presented, performed, and passed proficiently, yet lessons lacked the meaningful design and instructional execution required to extract each learner's *true* academic potential.

The missing link in the instructional strategy there was, well, *strategy*. Although there was a considerable amount of thoughtful planning among cross-curricular team members, it wasn't deemed necessary to collaborate within the same content area to determine purposeful instructional strategies based upon student needs. The apathetic mantra "If it isn't broken, don't fix it" seemed to apply, so time and energy were dedicated to promoting the affective domain while core teachers were left to their own devices to determine what worked and what didn't. Year after year, our test scores were among the highest in California, so minimal dialogue was exchanged regarding which teaching practices should be further implemented and which should be dissolved. According to the CST scores, we were successful, yet those numbers proved to be the district's largest nemesis. They prevented students' and teachers' *maximum* performance potential from being achieved.

Yes, even model schools have flaws. A school-wide strategic process implemented to guide instruction and maximize student achievement was the missing component necessary to reach new heights in teaching and learning.

The need for purpose-driven instruction extrapolated to a new level when I began teaching at Edison Middle School. Edison's demographics are shown in Figure 4.1.

My job description remained the same, yet expectations for students and teachers were far below par in comparison to that of my previous experience. What I had become accustomed to doing had to be drastically altered, as thematic units and cross-curricular activities were not implemented or embraced. As an

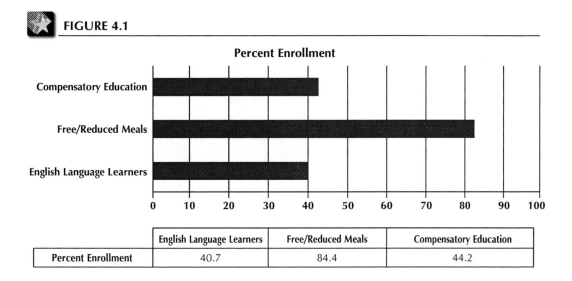

FIGURE 4.1

Percent Enrollment

	English Language Learners	Free/Reduced Meals	Compensatory Education
Percent Enrollment	40.7	84.4	44.2

unfortunate result, my crown grew even larger and heavier with my newfound independence; it was entirely up to me to create and execute an instructional practice that I deemed effective. Venturing beyond my own castle just wasn't necessary, as collaboration among colleagues was nonexistent unless a behavioral issue needed to be addressed. Student and teacher performance varied, as there were those who worked hard and others who hardly worked. Thus, California Standards Test results were unpredictable at best and were dependent upon classroom climate, with state standards being an optional point of reference as opposed to the foundation of sound instruction.

This practice remained the status quo, and test results spiraled downward at an alarming rate (Figure 4.2), landing our school in the No Child Left Behind Act's Program Improvement abyss.

This trend unfortunately continued until a new superintendent joined the district. His commitment to meaningful instruction and increased student achievement was evident upon his arrival. Skeptics scoffed and hopefuls dreamed as he delivered his vision of district reform by introducing components that would ultimately form the Data Teams process. We teachers raised eyebrows and commented under our breath as we questioned the journey on which we were about to embark. It was *our* all-encompassing journey; the new superintendent included himself, and seemed to place a special emphasis on the "team" component of "Data Team."

This administrative tactic instilled an immediate sense of unity, combined with a subtle undertone of guilt, driving the teachers who already worked hard to hang on his every word. Consequently, the few who "hardly worked" began a

 **FIGURE 4.2**

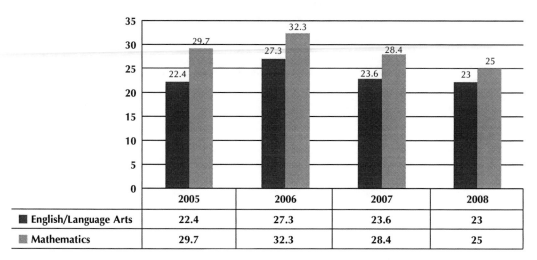

Edison Middle School—Percent Proficient

	2005	2006	2007	2008
■ English/Language Arts	22.4	27.3	23.6	23
▨ Mathematics	29.7	32.3	28.4	25

collaborative attempt at mutiny by combining an absence of accountability with apathy. They embraced all-too-familiar defeatist attitudes: "That won't work here"; "He obviously hasn't met our students"; "Is he aware that the reason our state test scores have tanked is because our English Language Learner population has increased?"

In spite of the division in teacher mindset, our new superintendent carried on with his conviction. He promised that the Data Teams process would prove effective, and made it quite clear that "those who were not on board would be left behind." His stand, though deemed somewhat threatening by "the resistance," was warmly welcomed by the majority. After all, we were tenacious, and we wanted our efforts to be evident in student success.

The information promoting Data Teams proved, without bias, that data doesn't lie; it simply reflects instructional practice. Thus, our superintendent's vision of reform was on its way to becoming a reality.

Our district's metamorphosis began as teachers collaborated to determine student strengths and weaknesses as indicated by the most recent California Standards Test results. State standards were then studied, which provided clarity as to exactly what our students needed to know and what our students needed to be able to do.

The next question we faced was "How?" How should students be taught based upon the findings? How do we best teach what we want our students to learn?

Although we desperately wanted students to improve and excel, did this new approach dare suggest that former policies, procedures, and favorite lessons be altered, drastically changed, or even eliminated?

Absolutely! Remember, the root word of teacher is "teach," and what has become comfortable instructional practice isn't always effective. The fact is, if students aren't learning, teachers aren't teaching. It's that simple. It's that harsh.

Therefore, we knew we needed to focus on what our findings were screaming, and we jumped head first into diligently determining grade-level and content-area goals and strategies.

We selected and focused on the standards that mattered most for student achievement, and collaborated with teachers who taught students in grade levels that preceded and followed those which we taught. We were given time to study the curricular alignment between grade levels and to discover areas of instruction that required more energy as well as those that weren't being addressed at all. The dialogue that occurred between colleagues was enlightening, and even included comments such as, "Man, I'm glad we looked at all of this. I always thought that *you* were supposed to be teaching that." We had been awakened from a deep, ignorant sleep. We were finally ready to put our new plans into action.

The data we collected and analyzed was foundational in developing SMART (Specific, Measurable, Achievable, Relevant, and Timely) goals that targeted a grade level, subject area, and our student population. Three research-based instructional strategies and results indicators (designed to monitor the effectiveness of strategies and implementation) were combined with a list of people responsible, necessary resources, and start and end dates (Figure 4.3). Once combined, plans became activated, and *all* teachers became accountable. The action plans, after all, were both created by and executed by the teachers, and were founded upon data that was undeniably factual. With that being the case, even "the resistance" was left grasping at straws to find a reason why they couldn't do what *they* had indicated needed to be done.

Whether student achievement goals were being met and data-driven Action Plans were being followed was determined by bi-quarterly Common Formative Assessments (CFAs). These assessments were written by grade-level or subject-area teachers to address student needs. They were intentionally aligned to our essential standards (Power Standards) and included both selected (multiple choice, true/false) and constructed (short or extended answer) response. These CFAs were accompanied by teacher-created rubrics that measured the students' responses and allowed for accurate and unbiased scoring. The data these CFAs provided allowed students to be viewed by a determination of strengths and weaknesses as opposed to a "performance level" indicated by the state tests. These frequent measurements

FIGURE 4.3

Action Plan Steps and Schedule

Content Area: Language Arts   Grade: 8   School: Edison Middle School

Targeted Goal 1 (what the students will do): Percentage of eighth-grade honors students scoring proficient and higher in Language Arts will increase from 89% to 95% by the end of of the 2009–2010 school year as measured by CST administered in April/May.

Strategies (What Adults Will Do)	Results Indicator (Measurement and Accountability Tool)	Persons Responsible, Resources, Start and End Dates
I will implement on a daily basis parts of speech, sentence structure, punctuation, and literary device. (practice–reinforcement): I will track comprehension via weekly quizzes and checking for understanding.	• If students are assessed weekly, areas of weakness within content areas will be determined. • If students practice correctness following further direct instruction, their assessment scores will increase. • If additional assessments are given to check for student understanding, their scores will increase.	**Dates:** September 2, 2009 through the end of April 2010. **Resources:** Core textbook; supplemental, standards-based material I will monitor assessment results and chart student progress.
• I will implement UNRAAVEL strategies. • I will provide each student with definitions for literary device, academic vocabulary, and parts of speech. • I will use CFA data to guide my instruction to increase student academic performance.	• If students use UNRAAVEL correctly and own academic language, then their CFA test scores will increase. • If I provide pre-test data to each student as a measurement device, students will be motivated to improve their CFA scores.	**Weekly Resources:** • UNRAAVEL poster • Composition books containing academic definitions • Individualized CFA data provided for each student
I will use academic vocabulary on a daily basis in conjunction with a progressive vocabulary wall.	If academic language is used on a daily basis, students will better understand the content of the CSTs and CFAs.	See above resources.

Edison School District 2009–2010

also allowed teachers to more accurately pinpoint student needs, and to provide differentiated instruction to promote learning as determined through the Data Teams process.

A CFA pre-test was given before instruction, and Data Teams collaborated by grade level or content area to collect and chart data, analyze strengths and obstacles, establish goals, select instructional strategies, and determine results indicators. Following instruction, the same CFA was given as a post-test, and Data Teams met again while adhering to the same structured format.

As a result of embracing this process, all of my students showed growth in their 2009 Language Arts California Standards Test scores when compared to 2008 (Figure 4.4). A significant number of students promoted to the next quintile, and some gained two quintiles. A few of my students skipped two quintiles entirely and gained three! This growth was consistent among students who entered my classes as far-below-basic and below-basic readers. It was also consistent among students who were designated English Language Learners within those classes.

FIGURE 4.4

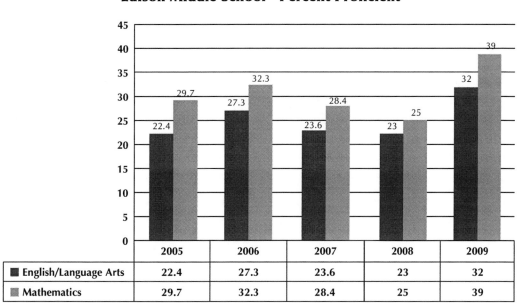

Edison Middle School—Percent Proficient

	2005	2006	2007	2008	2009
■ English/Language Arts	22.4	27.3	23.6	23	32
▦ Mathematics	29.7	32.3	28.4	25	39

Edison Middle School 2009 Post-Implementation Results

Although the Data Teams process may seem sterile and scientific, that is not a limitation. Rather, the process is artistically designed to open doors of communication—and we all know how heavy those castle doors can be!

During the process, it isn't unusual for teachers to venture into a discussion with another Data Team about strategies that have proven effective or failed miserably. What surfaces is obvious: sound teaching has no boundaries, and although the standards vary by grade level and content area, the art of teaching remains the same. That's right; the effective teaching strategies and bomb-proof lessons that have allowed us to earn our crowns are stolen and replicated, thus improving the learning experience of students beyond our classrooms.

Remember, students come into our schools wanting to succeed. When instruction isn't sound or differentiated to meet individual needs, or when assessments aren't fair and consistent, they feel as though they have been set up to fail. Even further, their desire to succeed likely diminishes. Students want to be assessed fairly and to receive timely feedback on their performance. This basic premise applies regardless of demographics.

The common denominator among my students is their unwavering desire to *own* what is taught to them and to push themselves toward academic proficiency and beyond. They know there is "method behind my madness," and that my expectations are honest and unbiased. They are fully aware that my instruction is driven by *their* data, and that a relevant rubric is used for assessment. Because the feedback on their Common Formative Assessments is timely, they know when to expect it. Therefore, it is not uncommon to find them waiting outside the classroom anxiously awaiting their results.

As with any new practice, initial student buy-in is contagious, and is based upon the enthusiasm and conviction of the teacher. Students want to please, and will rise to any sound level of expectation. Thus, it is the responsibility of the teacher to help each individual succeed.

By purposefully fusing the science and art of teaching, presentations and performances can remain an integral component of thematic units, cross-curricular assignments, and single-subject instruction. Successful state test scores can be a product of design rather than luck. The crowns that we so proudly donned can now be passed to our students, as they become empowered to reach their true potential.

Given this logical approach to promoting effective teaching practice and student achievement, let this be our new mantra: "If it doesn't work, analyze the data and fix it!"

WRITING MY SUCCESS STORY

As you reflect on Edison Middle School's success, take time to think about how their story applies to you in your current setting, and then answer the following questions:

1. *"Year after year, our test scores were among the highest in California, so minimal dialogue was exchanged regarding which teaching practices should be further implemented and which should be dissolved. According to the California Standards Test scores, we were successful, yet those numbers proved to be the district's largest nemesis."*

   These statements are all too often the result of schools that are "lucky," meaning they have high student achievement, but are not quite certain *how* they obtained their scores.

   Have you ever been part of a school or district that has been "lucky?" At the opposite end of the spectrum, have you been part of a school or district that has lost ground, and doesn't know why? Describe your experience.

   _____

   _____

   _____

   _____

   _____

2. *"Venturing beyond my own castle just wasn't necessary, as collaboration among colleagues was nonexistent unless a behavioral issue needed to be addressed."*

   The author describes the classrooms in her building as castles whose doors were not open to anyone else. Have you ever felt like this at your own site?

   _____

   _____

_____

_____

_____

3. *"That won't work here"; "He obviously hasn't met our students"; "Is he aware that the reason our California Standards Test scores have tanked is because our English Language Learner population has increased?"*

> One large obstacle in the change process can be a group of nay-sayers who believe they have tried the proposed method before, and already know it doesn't work. Have you ever worked with someone who had that mindset? Have you ever subscribed to that way of thinking? Is it possible to get the doubters on board with the school improvement process? If so, how can it be done?

_____

_____

_____

_____

_____

4. *"The fact is, if students aren't learning, teachers aren't teaching. It's that simple. It's that harsh."*

> This is a very powerful statement. Do you agree or disagree with the author?

_____

_____

_____

_____

_____

Gililland Middle School, Tempe, Arizona

"With the training and professional development that has occurred at Gililland Middle School during the last two years, teachers are analyzing and crunching data and taking their practices to a whole new level. They are now able to look at proficiency levels of students and determine if their instruction is effective based upon the numbers."

—Brady T. Wald, Assistant Principal

SUCCESSFUL CLIENT:	Gililland Middle School
LOCATION:	Tempe, Arizona (Urban)
POPULATION:	900 students
AUTHOR:	Brady T. Wald, M.Ed., Assistant Principal

The Change

Change is never easy for schools and districts to endure. Gililland Middle School continues to progress toward growth, a positive environment, academic achievement, a high level of rigor, and success. Four years ago, our school did not meet Adequate Yearly Progress under the No Child Left Behind Act, and was also labeled an "underperforming" school in the AZ LEARNS achievement profiles. We were targeted for corrective action, and were forced to change the focus of the school. Three new administrators were hired, and the turnover of teachers and classified staff was at a very high level. As a school, all stakeholders needed to have a plan of action, and specific, measurable goals had to be put in place to ensure that students and staff members would be successful.

Three Key Pieces of the Puzzle

As a school, we decided there were key focus areas that would drive the achievement, direction, and success of Gililland Middle School, and each student, teacher, and staff member held a crucial piece of the puzzle. We identified three important factors that we, as a school, could control. Putting these foundations in place has focused and driven our school toward high student engagement and increased academic achievement.

- **What we teach:** This refers to the curricula educators access to increase student achievement. Within their toolboxes are state standards, Big Ideas, Essential Questions, unit/lesson plans, curriculum maps, etc.

- **How we teach:** This embodies all the research-based strategies teachers use to increase student engagement and learning in the classrooms and school.

- **The environment in which we teach:** A positive learning environment is crucial to the success of a school. It allows students to learn and teachers to teach in a safe and collaborative atmosphere that ensures that *all* students will be successful.

The Administration's Responsibilities

Each stakeholder had a crucial role in changing Gililland Middle School. The administrators' responsibility at Gililland is to provide leadership and direction to the teachers and staff in order to achieve desired outcomes. One of our first goals was to develop a safe, positive learning environment where students could learn and teachers could teach. As a school, we focused on a school-wide discipline plan to establish the environment we were determined to obtain. In 2006, I was working as a "teacher on special assignment," and I knew my job was going to be extremely demanding. One of my major responsibilities was supporting teachers and resolving discipline issues. We developed an intervention program we called "the discipline matrix." This program allowed the entire school to have a consistent discipline model.

The support of teachers is crucial in creating a positive school environment. Each and every day that I come to work, I want to make sure that teachers and staff members know that they are appreciated and supported.

One way we continue to obtain that level of staff support is through visibility. Informal and formal walk-throughs are vital to a positive and safe learning environment for teachers and students. When we first started to conduct walk-throughs on a daily basis, teachers would stop teaching and ask what we wanted; they weren't used to seeing administrators and coaches walking through the classrooms. Students would turn their attention to the door to see who was coming through. Today, teachers continue to teach and students continue to learn despite sometimes seeing multiple people walking through the classrooms on any given day.

Teachers' Responsibilities

Three important factors led teachers at Gililland Middle School to shift their focus. First, once a positive and safe learning environment was established, teachers could focus on their teaching within the classroom. High expectations were placed on students, and those were reflected through the growth that took place in the classrooms. Teachers were able to apply research-based strategies that increased student engagement and achievement. Simple strategies such as exit tickets, think-pair-share, and Cloze reading were introduced to students to increase understanding and comprehension.

Second, teachers were able to use data to drive their instruction in the classroom. We started by taking a look at Northwest Evaluation Association (NWEA) test data. The NWEA test, given to students during the fall, winter, and spring, is a computer-based testing system built on thirty years of research. The assessment adapts to the students' responses, and makes adjustments according to their progress. This test is directly correlated with the state standardized test we administer every year, which allows our staff to have an understanding of the growth and progress our students are making throughout each term in reading, math, and science.

Finally, our master schedule allotted time for teachers to collaborate within their teams and departments, and each teacher was given an individual preparatory time as well. This allowed teachers to discuss strategies, coordinate and develop lesson plans, analyze data, and communicate about interventions and curriculum on a daily basis.

Students' Responsibilities

Students also had a major role in the growth and success of Gililland Middle School. They were asked to give 100 percent every day when they walked through the door, and to focus on learning. From day one, we communicated high standards. During the first week of each school year, we brought the students together in grade-level teams to discuss the expectations for the students, the teachers, and the school. The students would sit on the floor rather than in the bleachers, to provide close proximity. This exercise truly has brought our school together, immediately setting the tone for the entire school year.

A major goal we set for our students was to encourage them to graduate from high school and to attend and graduate from college. Many of our students would be the first in their family to attend a college or university. We established the excitement of this goal by inviting Arizona State University staff to our campus each year to talk about college life and opportunities.

One of the challenges we had to face was encouraging students to "buy in" to their learning. Each and every student is in control of his or her own actions and behaviors; they control their own destinies. As a school, we are constantly communicating the importance of testing and learning. Each teacher discusses the importance of the NWEA test before the students take it. The students are made aware that they will be placed in specific classes according to their assessment results. Teachers also discuss with students the fact that data will drive instruction by allowing monitoring that will result in adjustments to meet the needs of the kids in the classroom. Finally, students set growth goals before they take various assessments to create competition with themselves and to track their progress throughout the year.

Gililland Middle School: No Shame, No Blame, No Excuses

Gililland Middle School is a Title I school. We have approximately 900 students and more than 100 certified and classified staff members. Our school is considered an inner city school, and a high-needs school. We are a diverse school, in which many ethnicities and cultures are represented. Our demographics are described in Figure 5.1.

Currently, we are on an academic upward trend. In the past four years we have gone from a school that has not met Adequate Yearly Progress and has

FIGURE 5.1

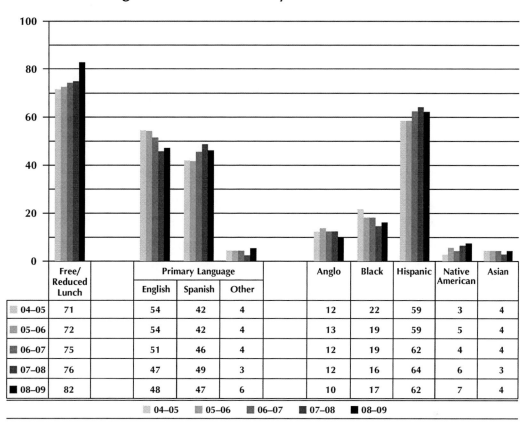

Percentage of Total Student Body at Gililland Middle School

	Free/ Reduced Lunch		Primary Language				Anglo	Black	Hispanic	Native American	Asian
			English	Spanish	Other						
04–05	71		54	42	4		12	22	59	3	4
05–06	72		54	42	4		13	19	59	5	4
06–07	75		51	46	4		12	19	62	4	4
07–08	76		47	49	3		12	16	64	6	3
08–09	82		48	47	6		10	17	62	7	4

04–05   05–06   06–07   07–08   08–09

underperformed, to meeting Adequate Yearly Progress and being labeled a "performing plus" school. This is an amazing accomplishment, but it did not happen immediately. We had to take it year by year, and continue to implement a school focus that would build for success.

As a staff, we established practices that were vital to our students' learning and that would dictate the needed growth and progress to improve achievement. We determined through a variety of resources and research that we would integrate the following into our instruction:

1. **Academic Vocabulary:** Tier 2 cross-curricular words students need to learn in-depth

2. **Content and Language Objectives (Big Ideas and Essential Questions):** Posted and communicated daily

3. **Technology:** Computers, smart boards, and response clickers to engage students

4. **Nonfiction Writing**

5. **80 Percent or Higher Level of Engagement:** Achieved in classrooms by using research-based strategies

Using Data to Drive Instruction: The Beginning

Data is essential to drive the instruction in the classroom, and it also provides an understanding of the direction the school is going. Initially, we were constantly analyzing data from our state standardized tests as well as our NWEA testing conducted three times per year. After my second year at Gililland Middle School, we decided to create a data wall that could be engaging and hands-on for teachers. Each student would be given a card with his or her state test data from Arizona's Instrument to Measure Standards Dual Purpose Assessment (AIMS DPA) and their NWEA reading and math data. The object was to identify, observe, and analyze the progress of each student, and to determine what type of strategies and interventions could be provided to meet the needs of each student.

After each NWEA testing session, teachers wrote the students' new scores on the wall to visualize progress. Teachers were taking ownership of their students' development by having the ability to personally move their kids' placement on the wall. In addition, each team and department established goals for the next round of testing. The goals for each group needed to be specific, measurable, and attainable. Most importantly, the success shown on the data walls and the specific goals needed to be communicated and shared with students, staff, district, parents, and community members.

After the second year of implementation of school goals and focus, we were starting to see dramatic results. Students, parents, the district, and the community were all excited and enthusiastic about the change and growth that Gililland Middle School was achieving. Despite our success, we could not just settle and become stagnant, so we asked, "How do we take it to the next level?"

Implementation of Common Formative Assessments and Data Teams

As a school, we decided the next level would be to introduce and implement Data Teams and Common Formative Assessments. To begin the process, we joined with one of our district's other middle schools (Fees Middle School) to train our leadership teams on Common Formative Assessments (CFAs) and Data Teams during the summer.

Next, the entire staff was formally trained by a consultant from The Leadership and Learning Center, with our school's leadership team involved for support. We felt the Common Formative Assessment training would go hand-in-hand with Data Teams training, because teachers would be looking at data from the CFAs to drive instruction.

Since the first day of training, the Data Teams process has been ongoing. Like anything you want to become better at in life or within your profession, you have to practice a procedure or routine several times before it becomes successful and you're good at it. We have experienced speed bumps along the road to implementation, such as negativity and push-back. However, it was tremendously easy for us as leaders to provide evidence of improvement, growth, and perseverance among staff members, which helped to get everyone on board with the process.

Along with practice, teachers and administrators need time and consistency. Each of our departments meets three days a week to discuss the development and implementation of Common Formative Assessments, data from CFAs, curriculum maps, unit plans, lesson plans, Big Ideas, Essential Questions, and differentiation in the classroom.

The leadership role throughout the entire implementation of the CFA/Data Teams process has been staying ahead and on top of the learning curve. As leaders, it is crucial that we are able to provide support by answering and asking questions, giving guidance and direction, and allowing teachers to voice feedback and concerns in the process. Also, it is vital to be knowledgeable about the most up-to-date research pertaining to the Data Teams process and CFAs.

The best way to maintain familiarity with the Data Teams process and how it is being used in your school is to actually take part in the Data Team meetings. As leaders, we should strive to work together collaboratively with teachers so that we all get the feel of the Data Teams process. A leadership presence shows teachers that the Data Teams process is vital to the success of the students and school, and that their participation in the process is valued. We attend departmental meetings, professional development trainings, and work alongside our staff in the implementation process.

Our district, Tempe Elementary School District 3, put together an extensive curriculum map that includes a blueprint for each content area. In 2008, curriculum maps were developed by groups of teachers in each content area that met throughout the entire year. These maps contain Big Ideas, Essential Questions, key vocabulary, and assessments. This procedure has had a positive effect in aligning teachers' instruction. We have utilized the curriculum map in helping us develop the CFAs for each unit that is being taught.

Working with CFAs and Data Teams for an entire year was extremely positive for our teachers, as they were already trained and comfortable with the process. Each department within each grade level has been responsible for writing a unit plan collaboratively. Once the unit plan process is complete, then individual teachers can begin the development of their formal lesson plans using a school-wide template.

Providing support has been a key ingredient in the success of Data Teams and CFAs at Gililland Middle School. Inviting consultants from The Leadership and Learning Center to facilitate and support our staff has been extremely beneficial. In order to make this happen, we used school improvement money, and applied for a variety of grants through the state to help us pay for that support. We were very fortunate to have Juan Cordova, Connie Kamm, Jan Christinson, and Lisa Almeida, Professional Development Associates from The Leadership and Learning Center, support not only the teachers at Gililland Middle School, but also the administrators and coaches. Lisa and Jan have been visiting our school every month for the past two years. They have focused on a variety of topics with our staff such as the Data Teams process, developing Common Formative Assessments, and identifying Big Ideas using curriculum maps, as well as the differentiation of instruction to ensure that all students are becoming proficient.

Team and Department Collaboration

Accountability and communication are essential to the life spans of practices such as Common Formative Assessments and Data Teams. All of the focus areas previously mentioned are central to the success of our school. This year, we developed a departmental focus form that each department is required to complete by the end of the week and then send to the administration electronically. This form contains the Big Ideas being discussed, the focus of the meeting, meeting minutes, and teacher roles, as well as the Data Teams process. Also, teams and departments can identify students or analyze proficiency data from each class or teacher. In addition to the Data Teams component, there are other discussions taking place within the meetings. This form allows for teams to communicate what is being discussed, such as strategies, interventions, data, unit/lesson plans, etc.

Our elective subjects team (physical education, industrial arts, intervention, Spanish, art, and music) and departments are exceeding expectations with this whole process. Each week, a different group of elective teachers presents to their colleagues an engagement or instructional strategy that they can use immediately in the classroom to boost student achievement. They also present a quick article and PowerPoint presentation on research-based strategies and curriculum from the core classes that they can integrate into their own lessons. These types of activities are so powerful and exciting to be a part of. Teachers are seeing their hard work and dedication to students paying off.

With the training and professional development that has occurred at Gililland Middle School during the last two years, teachers are analyzing and crunching data and taking their practices to a whole new level. They are now able to look at proficiency levels of students and determine if their instruction is effective based upon the numbers.

Small-group instruction and identifying specific needs of students has been very challenging at the middle school level. We are asking more and more teachers to take the time, using small-group instruction, to teach and re-teach the students that our Data Teams have identified as needing extra help. Differentiation in the classroom is a key component to the percentage of proficient students a teacher will have in his or her classroom. One question always asked is: "What do I do for the students who are already proficient?" There are several ways to enrich those particular students. At Gililland Middle School, students who need continuous enrichment are just as important as the students to which we provide intervention or small-group instruction. The varied needs of students are why differentiation and rigor in the classroom are so important.

A powerful tool that we are using is the student tracking sheet (shown at the end of this chapter). Dr. Robert Marzano's research shows that students tracking their own progress can have significant gains in achievement scores. Based on Dr. Marzano's research, we devised a data sheet that students can use to chart their own progress (Figure 5.2). We have used a similar tool in the past with NWEA testing, but because we are implementing Common Formative Assessments in all of our classrooms, this became a resource that teachers could use for students to track students' progress on all assessments in the classroom. Each student can graph their pre- and post-CFA progress, hopefully seeing a drastic increase in the proficiency level of their scores. The same kind of tracking is done on the same page for the state standardized test, NWEA tests, and benchmark assessments.

Technology has been another tool that we continue to use at Gililland. We utilized a grant this year to purchase a set of response clickers (devices that allow students to respond to questions with hand-held "clickers" that are attached to a system that immediately compiles the students' responses) for every classroom. The students are 100 percent engaged in these types of activities. Using these tools, students are able to take a Common Formative Assessment, summative assessment, etc. in a creative and exciting way. The results are posted for the teacher and students immediately. They can then use the data to determine which students are proficient, or need additional instruction in a given area. This type of information

FIGURE 5.2

Keeping Track of My Learning at Gililland Middle School

Common Formative Assessments will INCREASE Your NWEA & AIMS scores!

Name: _____   Teacher: _____   Grade: _____

My goal on each Common Formative Assessment is to be 80 percent proficient

Specific strategies that I am going to use to attain my CFA goals are:

AIMS 2009:	Reading _____	Writing _____	Math _____	Science _____
Fall NWEA:	Reading _____	Math _____	Language _____	
Winter NWEA:	Reading _____	Math _____	Language _____	
Spring NWEA:	Reading _____	Math _____		

> **EXCEEDS = 85% AND ABOVE**
> **MEETS = 75%–84%**
> **APPROACHES = 51%–74%**
> **FALLS FAR BELOW = 50% AND BELOW**

CFA Topics	100% 90% 80% 70% 60% 50% 40% 30% 20% 10% 0%									
	CFA #1	CFA #2	CFA #3	CFA #4	CFA #5	CFA #6	CFA #7	CFA #8	CFA #9	CFA #10

allows teachers to monitor and adjust their instruction based on the responses from the students.

Building Capacity within Gililland Middle School

A strategy we implemented this year at our school is to something we call CFA/Data Team facilitators. We identified a group of teachers from each department and grade level to be represented at administration meetings. Our goal was to have a group of facilitators take the information presented at the administration meetings back to their departments and teams. This also became a way to hear concerns about or issues with the CFA or Data Teams process and figure out a solution, rather than allowing it to remain a problem that festers within the school. Teams or departments could have questions about the process, or something might not be working. The facilitators can take those questions and pose them to the rest of the group to seek a solution to the issue. Using facilitators is a fantastic way to communicate, discuss, and analyze issues, knowing that the information presented will then be discussed with the teams and departments within days.

We have one staff meeting per month in which we address a variety of strategies, issues, information, and concerns. At each meeting, we have different teachers that present educational topics and strategies that our school can use to increase student achievement. We have discussed topics such as positive specific feedback, tracking student progress, academic vocabulary, using games to boost achievement, and many more.

Celebrating Results and Success

The success at Gililland Middle School has been astounding; we have so much to be excited about regarding student growth and achievement. Our NWEA average Rausch Unit (RIT) scores and growth have been significant in our student body. Because of the specific and immediate feedback that students are receiving in the classrooms and testing environments, our typical annual growth on the NWEA has been three to four RIT score points (Figure 5.3). The teachers are stressing the importance of using data to drive their instruction in the classroom to meet the needs of all students. Also, teachers are learning new strategies and effectively putting them in place to ensure that students are engaged and striving toward excellence in the classroom.

Another accomplishment in the past three years has been our change in status from an "underperforming" school to a "performing plus" school. The hard work and dedication of the staff at Gililland Middle School has been truly amazing.

FIGURE 5.3

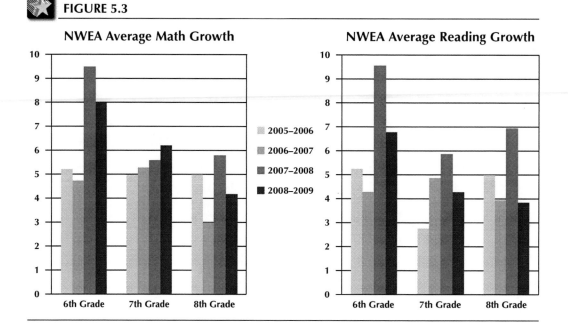

Every year, there have been significant changes and new programs that were implemented. The staff took on those specific challenges and met all expectations. As a school, our math and reading scores continue to grow each and every year.

Gililland continues to work toward achieving Adequate Yearly Progress. We achieved our goals for the 2008–2009 school year (Figures 5.4 and 5.5). All of the building blocks that have been implemented—CFAs, Data Teams, curriculum maps, unit and lesson plans, and team/department collaborations—continue to play a part in the determination and perseverance of this school. Instead of becoming complacent because of the great results that we have seen, we are always trying to continue to build and grow academically by taking it to the next level.

We are enthusiastic, optimistic, and hopeful about the continuous improvement and development of our students and staff. These changes did not happen immediately, nor did they happen flawlessly. Change happens gradually, and results improve in due time. And we did not succeed because of any particular individual, but because we worked as a team. Helen Keller said it best: "Alone we can do so little, together we can do so much." At Gilliland we teach, learn, and achieve through the acronym used in Mark Sanborn's *The Encore Effect* (2008): "T.E.A.M.—Together Everyone Achieves More." We are truly a team that works together for the growth, achievement, and success of *all* students.

FIGURE 5.4

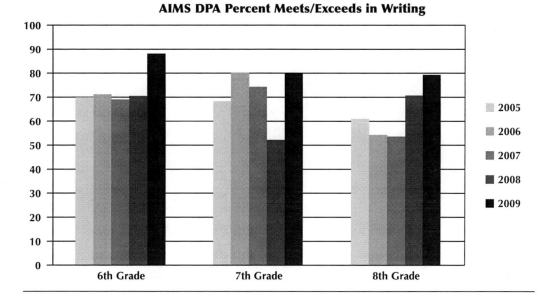

AIMS DPA Percent Meets/Exceeds in Writing

FIGURE 5.5

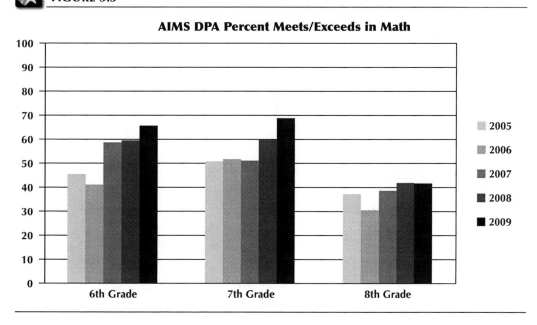

AIMS DPA Percent Meets/Exceeds in Math

**Gilliland Middle School
Data Teams in action.**

WRITING MY SUCCESS STORY

As you reflect on Gililland Middle School's success, take time to think about how their story applies to you in your current setting, and then answer the following questions:

1. The author stated, *"Most importantly, the success shown on the data walls and the specific goals needed to be communicated and shared with students, staff, district, parents, and community members."*

> Clear accountability to all stakeholders is critical to school growth and improvement. Where is your district or site in the process of goal-setting and presenting objectives in a clear and transparent way to the community (students, teachers, parents, etc.)?

_____

_____

_____

_____

_____

2. *"Along with practice, teachers and administrators need time and consistency."*

> It seems as though time is a rare commodity in education. Do you often feel stressed or pressured for time? What strategies could you immediately put into effect that would free up more time in your daily routine to focus on essential practices?

_____

_____

_____

_____

_____

3. The author mentions that the staff was trained in Common Formative Assessments and Data Teams around the same time. He says that these two processes go hand in hand.

What Common Formative Assessment practices are currently used in your classroom, school, or district? Are they connected loosely or seamlessly to your Data-Driven Decision Making practices?

_____

_____

_____

_____

_____

4. *"Each week, a different group of elective teachers presents to their colleagues an engagement or instructional strategy that they can use immediately in the classroom to boost student achievement."*

What forum(s) do you have at your location that empower(s) educators to share best practices with each other? How often do these types of discussions occur?

_____

_____

_____

_____

_____

SUCCESS STORY SIX

Elkhart Community Schools, Elkhart, Indiana

"Recently, our principals were asked by the superintendent, 'What is most significant about our work that we must retain in light of impending budget cuts?' Their response was, 'Data Teams.'"

—Dr. John R. Hill, Director of Curriculum and Instruction

SUCCESSFUL CLIENT:	Elkhart Community Schools
LOCATION:	Elkhart, Indiana (North-Central Indiana, Suburban)
POPULATION:	13,000 students
AUTHOR:	Dr. John R. Hill, Director of Curriculum and Instruction

At Elkhart Community Schools, our path to collaboration began with a simple phone call in the winter of 2004. That phone call led to a surprising conversation, an initial engagement, professional development planning, lofty goal-setting, and a journey not yet complete that has created empowered and collaborative educators in our district.

In the fall of 2004, several Elkhart Community Schools central office and building administrators met in a "superintendent's cabinet" meeting to discuss and plan for the annual administrators' retreat. We quickly agreed that we needed to depart from the format of the past—single isolated sessions with no interconnections and no follow-up activity. What we needed was a connected series of professional development trainings centered on a set of specific topics that required frequent and regular follow-up. We began looking for an outside entity that might partner with Elkhart Community Schools for the long term. A couple of suggestions about potential partners were made, and I agreed to make initial contacts, as I had made hundreds, maybe thousands, of phone calls to schools and entities that do business with schools during my career.

I called the number I had been given for Dr. Douglas Reeves, expecting the normal greeting from a secretary on the other end of the line. After a couple of rings, however, I was startled by the simple response, "This is Doug Reeves." I recovered from my surprise quickly enough to have a decent first conversation with Dr. Reeves about Elkhart Community Schools' desire to build a long-term commitment with a consulting group to provide professional development for our administrators. He said that it was good that we were seeking a long-term commitment. What followed challenged Elkhart Community Schools to develop a much more sophisticated plan and loftier goals.

Two of us from the district's central office were invited to attend a face-to-face professional development planning session held at The Leadership and Learning Center (then the Center for Performance Assessment) in Englewood, Colorado. We met with an entourage of The Center's staff, including Dr. Douglas Reeves, to begin the process of determining our needs and expanding our understanding about what exactly we wanted to accomplish. Our focus became more accurately fixed on providing professional development for *all* teachers and administrators, building our internal capacity to continue that professional development, and establishing a cadre of teachers and administrators who would begin practicing what had been learned during the professional development sessions.

Establishing the Baseline

As a result of the planning session at The Center, our district decided to have teachers and administrators complete a basic series of workshops organized and facilitated by both The Center's professional development staff and by our own staff, who were gradually gaining the certification needed to facilitate The Center's workshops. Specifically, the three workshops included Data Teams, Effective Teaching Strategies, and Making Standards Work.

The first stage included having most administrators complete the Data Teams workshop, conducted on-site by Tony Flach, a Professional Development Associate from The Center. In January of 2005, two of us attended certification training in

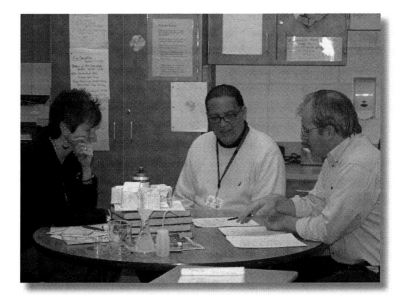

Data Teams and Data-Driven Decision Making in Denver, Colorado. We were very aware that the realization of our goals depended on us obtaining the necessary information, understanding the processes, and learning the art of workshop facilitation. Adding to the importance and urgency of our training was the fact that the first workshops for our district's teachers were already scheduled to begin in February, a few short weeks away. After achieving the required certification, the workshops were conducted as scheduled, and the first few groups of teachers returned to their schools with a modest commitment to "give this team thing a try." Because of our limited internal capacity to hold many workshops in a short period of time, our initial progress was rather sporadic and slow. We observed the valiant efforts of a few teams, but it was difficult getting people started, and then helping them, when their first attempts at using Data Teams did not produce much of anything, except for the frustration of learning something new and not being very good at it.

Then, a letter arrived that changed everything. Master teachers wear many hats in the field of education; sometimes they represent their colleagues as president of the local teacher's union, or they sometimes serve as the superintendent. We were indeed fortunate to have master teachers in both capacities; Sara Wood as President of the Elkhart Teachers Association and Mark Mow as Superintendent. Master teachers understand that learners learn better by observing action rather than hearing a lecture. If we were going to strongly advocate for collaboration—the heart of Data Teams work—then collaboration had to be demonstrated, rather than just spoken about. The superintendent and the president of the Elkhart Teachers

Association together drafted and signed a letter requiring all of our district's teachers and instructional administrators to complete the three basic workshops by no later than the summer of 2007.

This communication resulted in a challenge; we had to create ways to accomplish the task of training everyone, when Elkhart Community Schools employs more than 1,000 teachers and instructional administrators. The three required workshops involved six total days of professional development time. That calculates out to 6,000 "person days" of professional development to be completed in about two and a half years. I remembered the words of a former superintendent, who concluded most strategy meetings with the command: "Let's go out and make it happen."

"Make it happen" is just what we did. By the summer of 2007, we attained completion of the three workshops by all teachers and instructional administrators. We also had approximately fifty educators who received certification in at least one of the workshop areas. This cadre of certified educators continues to provide workshop facilitation and collegial support within our district. As we neared the completion date of the summer workshops in 2007, our thoughts turned to what would follow on our projected timeline. We turned again to The Leadership and Learning Center to help us establish the direction and timeline.

Beyond the Workshops

Three of us representing the Elkhart Community Schools central office again traveled to The Center in Denver to discuss potential follow-up to the workshops. Our own experience with sophisticated models of professional development provided part of

the answer as well. That experience led us to believe that placing educators who completed the workshops back into the real world of the classroom without continued support would severely reduce the potential effect of the professional development. Teachers not getting a sufficient amount of implementation support could even lead to the total disappearance of the skills learned in the workshops.

Fortunately, The Leadership and Learning Center staff has exactly the same view of sustaining and building capacity from initial workshop completion to actual implementation. Our meetings in Denver with The Center staff, Dr. Douglas Reeves included, focused on what we could support on our own and what The Center staff could support with periodic on-site visits. I remember Dr. Reeves' spoken message, one that he has recorded in writing as well: "Unless you are paying close attention to the monitoring of implementation, the value of massive amounts of professional development may be totally lost." Our implementation collaboration with The Center has continued from its beginnings in the fall of 2007 through the current 2009–2010 school year.

For our own part, we divided our schools (twenty buildings) between four district curriculum and instruction administrators. Each administrator works directly with the principal and leadership team, meeting at least monthly to provide feedback, suggestions, and discussion on implementation of Data Teams, effective teaching practices, and "unwrapping" and embedding academic standards. As we approached the beginning of the 2008–2009 academic year, Elkhart Community Schools and the Elkhart Teachers Association agreed upon adding a compensated extra-duty line to all teacher contracts for a minimum of ten one-hour Data Team meetings over the course of the academic year. With the advent of contract expectations for each teacher, including pay for extra time, Data Teams began meeting across the district in a much more uniform and consistent pattern than in the previous school years.

In addition, during the same school year, we created principals' Data Teams organized around the same four clusters of schools served by one curriculum and instruction administrator. The principals' Data Teams meet once a month during the school year, with a member of The Center's consulting staff (Dr. Ray Smith or Dr. Angela Peery) and our curriculum and instruction administrator. Built into this design is a mid-year and end-of-year status report on implementation progress by each principal. The superintendent is present for the mid-year and end-of-year status reports, which are delivered orally and in brief written format. Progress made is gauged by the Data Teams process, creation and use of common assessments, and collaboration, (with evidence collected to substantiate the rubric placement of each Data Team in each school).

Collaboration—It's What We Do!

While it is important that we are able to write about our collaborative efforts, it is of far greater significance that we reflect on our collaborative actions as teams of educators. If our business is all about collaboration, then we have to continue to enhance our culture of teamwork to higher levels—no one makes decisions alone, and no one acts alone.

We remain engaged in taking this concept from a few high-performance teams to *all* of our teams at both the teacher and administrative level. We remain stead-fast, with a solid commitment that we will do whatever it takes, for as long as it

FIGURE 6.1

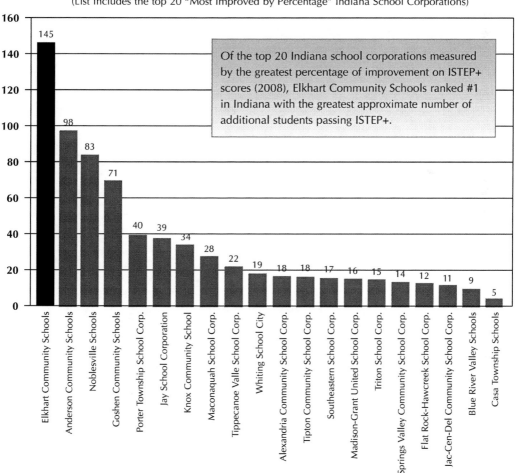

Most Improved by Approximate Number of Students, 2008

(List includes the top 20 "Most Improved by Percentage" Indiana School Corporations)

Of the top 20 Indiana school corporations measured by the greatest percentage of improvement on ISTEP+ scores (2008), Elkhart Community Schools ranked #1 in Indiana with the greatest approximate number of additional students passing ISTEP+.

takes, to grow and then maintain a collaborative culture. We have recently reached a milestone on this journey that we believe is significant. Elkhart Community Schools has accomplished a growth curve unsurpassed by other schools, not just within a single school or a few schools, but within the entire K–12 population (Figure 6.1). This is a direct result of the decision we made five years ago to involve every teacher and instructional administrator in a comprehensive professional development plan, and the corresponding implementation plan that has enabled the entire district to advance as a unit. To continue the necessary work and refinement, we expect to progress as a unit, not by individual schools, individual teams, or individual teachers.

Celebrating our Success

As we began the 2009–2010 school year, principals, assistants, and central office administrators took a moment to celebrate the growth of our students with the Memorial High School marching band drum line and a large cake distributed piece by piece to all. From the central office, the message was sent to each building administrator that a celebration was appropriate in each of their schools for the staff members who have worked diligently to learn and apply new strategies, to fully implement collaborative team practices, and, ultimately, to begin improving the academic trajectory of our students. We were able to attend several such celebrations in individual schools as the staff reported to their buildings to prepare for the arrival of their students in August 2009.

The messages sent from the state and from local district leaders can sometimes be perceived as conflicting. The state seems to be perpetually indicating that public schools are not achieving desired results with students. At the same time, we sincerely believe that significant growth in student achievement, as measured by the Indiana Statewide Testing for Education Progress—Plus (ISTEP+) assessments over a three-year period, has been attained in Elkhart Community Schools. Thus, the question is raised, "Who is right?" One perspective, negating the need to take sides over the matter, is that both positions have merit. We believe that more can and should be done to help more of our students achieve and grow in their academic endeavors. To that end, we have not yet achieved everything we are capable of achieving as educators. We also believe, however, that there is something substantial to celebrate; something to stand up and cheer about. More of our students are passing the ISTEP+ as a result of our concerted efforts to help them accomplish academic success. We are not discounting either position, but recognizing that both statements can be useful to Elkhart Community Schools.

Our educators will continue to celebrate the accomplishments and progress we have made. We know that we can support our celebrations with data. We also know it is a journey to improve over time; not a sprint-style race. If we continue to help our students improve, then the slow steady climb is worthy of celebration. *How* we accomplished the improvements—gathering the cause data, if you will—is also worthy. It is because we measure and record the cause data that we have a greater likelihood of continuing our progress and sustaining that progress in the future.

There are also several additional reasons to celebrate. One of our high schools has instituted a freshman academy this year, which required a redesign of the teacher Data Teams from a departmental structure to cross-subject area teams working with the same set of freshman students. One of the major academic targets established to begin this year was increasing the number of freshman students who earned ten or more academic credits by the conclusion of the school year. The numbers at the end of the first semester indicated that 85 percent of the 433 freshman students had received academic credit that kept them on track to earn those ten or more credits. So, what would there be to celebrate in this isolated data set? The high school administrators studied the research about specific factors that place students at risk for not achieving high school graduation on time. One such factor is not achieving sufficient academic credits during their freshman year. High school administrators shared aspects of their study with the freshman academy teacher teams and then asked the question, "What can each of your teams do this year to improve the chances that more of your students will remain on track for graduation?" Thanks, in large part, to their Data Teams structure, the freshman academy teams could provide weekly feedback to students who were behind in their assigned work, or for those students who were not participating in the classroom. Many of the students, once made aware they were slipping toward unsuccessful completion of coursework, began to get their assignments up-to-date and to participate more fully in the classroom. For many of these students, the semester concluded with the awarding of credit in classes, rather than the dismal notice of failure for reasons that were entirely addressable by the students.

When we claim we have changed the culture of Elkhart Community Schools, we intend to say that our teachers and administrators have changed the culture of teaching and learning to one they consciously control. Educator efficacy has been raised to levels thought unattainable a short time ago. Recently, our principals were asked by the superintendent, "What is most significant about our work that we must retain in light of impending budget cuts?" Their response was, "Data Teams."

I would like to thank Mark Mow, Superintendent; Tom Neat, Assistant Superintendent; and members of the Elkhart Community Schools Board of Education for their deep understanding of this collaborative project, and for their continued support as we venture on ahead. Also, thanks are extended to Brad Sheppard, Dave Benak, and Dave McGuire in the curriculum and instruction office—they make our collaboration successful on a daily basis. Thanks are also due to our building principals and teacher teams, who continue to refine both their knowledge of and skill in collaboration. Finally, thanks to Dr. Douglas Reeves and the staff at The Leadership and Learning Center, who complete our collaborative team. Our journey together has been instructive and beneficial, and together we have helped our students realize more of their academic potential.

WRITING MY SUCCESS STORY

As you reflect on the success of Elkhart Community Schools, take time to think about how their story applies to you in your current setting, and then answer the following questions:

1. The author continually talks about the importance of collaboration. This belief is highlighted in the following statement: *"We remain steadfast, with a solid commitment that we will do whatever it takes, for as long as it takes, to grow and then maintain a collaborative culture."*

    How would you rate the level of collaboration within your team, school, or district? What can be done to improve this status?

    _____

    _____

    _____

    _____

    _____

2. *"We also know it is a journey to improve over time; not a sprint-style race."*

    What elements of the Elkhart Community Schools story illustrate this notion? Would you describe your current school improvement process as a sprint or a marathon? Explain.

    _____

    _____

    _____

    _____

    _____

3. The author states that *how* (the cause data) the district made these
   improvements is as important as the results they achieved.

   Why is it critical to focus on the journey, and not just the prize?

   _____

   _____

   _____

   _____

   _____

Marylin Avenue Elementary School, Livermore, California

"Because of the Data Teams process, our culture, our values and beliefs, and the actions and behaviors of staff members have changed. We've experienced a shift in focus from teacher needs to student needs. Individual students and their instructional needs are now discussed at every meeting. Strategies are selected that will help a student evolve. Each week, student progress is reviewed. This collaboration has made every teacher at the table aware of our collective investment in all students at all grade levels."

—Jeffrey Keller, Principal

SUCCESSFUL CLIENT:	Marylin Avenue Elementary School
LOCATION:	Livermore, California (Suburban)
POPULATION:	510 students (64 percent English Language Learners)
AUTHOR:	Jeffrey Keller, Principal

Marylin Avenue Elementary School's arduous four-year journey from "underperforming" and identified for Program Improvement under the No Child Left Behind Act, to a district model for improved student achievement, is a remarkable one. It demonstrates the perseverance of our educators. And, as any staff member at Marylin will tell you, our progress would not have been possible without the implementation of the Data Teams process. The story of our school's transformation is all the more remarkable when the demographics of the community it serves are considered.

Background and Demographics

For a number of years, the population at our 52-year-old Title I neighborhood school had been changing. The number of English Language Learners, the number of Hispanic students, and the number of children living in poverty increased dramatically. In the 2001–2002 school year, 33 percent of our students qualified for free or reduced lunches. That number has increased to 84 percent. In 2001–2002, 46 percent of our students were English Language Learners. That number is currently 64 percent. The Hispanic population in our school has increased from 36 percent to 76 percent in the same time. The white population was 42 percent in the 2001–2002 school year, and it is now 14 percent. The open enrollment policy in our district contributed to the change in our school's demographics. During this period of demographic change, our test scores were continuously declining.

While following the methods and recommendations of the best minds in educational reform might seem straightforward, the work of cultural and behavioral change requires an unwavering commitment, and years to accomplish. All of the classroom teachers currently at our school have embraced this change in their work and willingly endured the labor needed to make it a reality. We are an excellent example of successful change made possible by "different practices, leadership, and commitment—not just different people," (Reeves, *Leading Change in Your School*, 2009).

We realize we have much more to learn and to do, and we are continually expanding our knowledge base and the collective confidence that comes with that knowledge. Yet challenges remain; many of our students are too far below grade-level standards. Equity for all students remains a constant goal, but we would like to share the story of what we have accomplished so far, and how we did it.

In 1999, Marylin Avenue Elementary School was identified as "underper-forming" by the Immediate Intervention/Underperforming Schools Program (II/USP), part of California's Public Schools Accountability Act. Experts in under-performance were called in to help bring about the change needed to improve student achievement. A dedicated group of educators at Marylin wanted to know more so they could do better by their students, and so began the work of reform.

Under the leadership of the previous administrator and his lead teachers, who continue to teach here, a new leadership team was put in place. Teachers were required to use the district's adopted texts and programs such as Open Court and Accelerated Math. In addition, a school-wide series of language arts assessments (literacy battery) was adopted. "Sacred" time for literacy instruction and for teacher collaboration became an integral part of the school day. Some teachers began to question the way things had been done.

Marylin Avenue Elementary School also built a partnership with a high-performing, but demographically very different, school across town, Almond Avenue Elementary School. Almond, targeted for closure by the district administration due to budgetary considerations, had been undergoing its own reform. At our respective sites, our schools pursued "best practices" for student learning, but it wasn't until the school closed that the staffs of these two schools merged. A core group from Almond asked to be assigned to Marylin because of the schools' allegiance to common educational ideals. One year after that, Marylin Avenue Elementary School welcomed a new principal, and the second phase of reform began.

When I began serving as principal at Marylin Avenue Elementary School, I found colleagues who were working very hard to do their individual and collective best for the students. Yet, this new role I had taken as an educator, and the responsibilities that came with it, had me observing Marylin through new eyes. This is what I saw, and what was still in question:

- We were committed to standards-based instruction, but did we all agree on what that means?

- Did we agree on how to manage the large number of standards included in California's framework?

- How did individuals and teams decide on which standards deserved deep attention? Did they try to identify essential standards at all?

- We were committed to a common literacy assessment battery, but were we making effective use of the data we collected?

- Did we know how to gather and interpret our data so that we knew how effective we were instructionally?

- We were committed to teacher collaboration, but what were we "co-laboring" about? Was it lunchroom procedures, or lessons constructed for learning? Was it field trips, or fact-finding around student data? Was it activities, or the selection of anchor papers in writing?

- We were committed to shared leadership, but what were we sharing?
- Was the focus of collaboration playground rules, lunchroom behavior, and the tidiness of the staff room, or was it student data, goals, and best practices?
- Was there a plan in place to ensure that students learn?

All of these good questions were worthy of our attention, but our attention was frequently diverted by remodeling our site, school culture, and climate.

Putting Out the Fire

In the fall of 2006, Marylin Avenue Elementary School was identified for Program Improvement under the No Child Left Behind Act. Along with that designation came a sense of urgency among teachers and support staff that attention was needed to address the changing demographics and resulting challenges. The "house was on fire," and we needed immediate plans and actions to demonstrate improvement, or we would have to face the consequences.

We were encouraged to follow the adopted reading program Open Court page by page, and it was strongly recommended that we use the district report card to determine our essential standards. Despite this pressure from the county and district, we held strong to our belief in our ability to follow the research that accentuated practices for effective school reform. Fortunately, district administration granted us the flexibility to create our own plan for improvement. This tenacity and determination ultimately led to our decision to implement the Data Teams process. The case study of 90/90/90 schools by Dr. Douglas Reeves, and my fifteen-minute meeting with Dr. Reeves during The Leadership and Learning Center's Senior Leadership Institute in the fall of 2006 were key factors in this decision.

Getting Excited About Change

The foundation was laid for collaborating as grade-level teams. Although our focus was not on student achievement and data, we knew agendas and norms were critical to effective meetings. We were about to learn their importance in the Data Teams process. Having an established leadership team provided the structure to hold conversations as a staff.

While many of us were reading books and articles about school improvement and instructional practices, it was Dr. Reeves' 90/90/90 study, read by our whole staff during the fall of 2005, that had a profound and lasting effect. This article helped us realize that schools with similar populations to ours can achieve at higher levels. We learned that this requires a process that focuses teachers on student achievement by collaboratively analyzing data from common and frequent assessments. My mantra of "common frequent assessments" was revised to Common Formative Assessments (CFAs) as we learned more.

After reading this article, we wanted to know everything about what effective schools were doing. This article sparked a flurry of exchanges at the staff room table as we began to read voraciously. Articles and books by Douglas Reeves, Robert Marzano, Michael Schmoker, and Victoria Bernhardt were underlined, written in, highlighted, and plastered with questions and comments on sticky notes. Our shared knowledge was growing, as well as the breadth of our questions.

In July 2006, the leadership team made the decision to send me, five teachers, and an information technology administrator to Chico, California, to attend the Education for the Future Institute, led by Victoria Bernhardt, with the intention of learning how to use and analyze multiple sources of data. We came back armed with the tools to build a framework for continuous improvement.

When we returned to school in August 2006, we began to implement that process faithfully, beginning with revisiting our mission and developing the first draft of our shared vision. We used a "root-cause analysis tool" to examine the reasons our scores were declining, and to develop an action plan with SMART (Specific, Measurable, Achievable, Relevant, and Timely) goals and strategies to help us address student achievement.

With the help of Just for the Kids—California (an organization dedicated to school improvement, largely funded by United Way), we had the opportunity to hold conference calls and to visit schools with similar populations during the fall of 2006. At Ralph Bunche Elementary School in Compton, California, we watched a Data Team in action. Teachers were collecting data every two weeks and the school was celebrating student achievement regularly.

In November 2006, I attended the Senior Leadership Institute in Cambridge, Massachusetts, hosted by The Leadership and Learning Center. There, I learned the importance of a leader's actions and behavior, and the direct impact of my actions as principal on student achievement. While at this conference, I asked if Dr. Reeves would take a few minutes to look over our newly adopted school plan (all twelve pages). During this quick conversation, Dr. Reeves told me that if Marylin Avenue Elementary School wanted to see gains in student achievement that school year, we needed to get going with the Data Teams process immediately. I called our staff members from Cambridge to convey Dr. Reeves' advice, and returned to school with even more evidence that supported the implementation of the Data Teams process.

Making the Leap to Data Teams

The work accomplished in the early fall of 2006 laid the groundwork for a change in behavior and attitude. Talk of CFAs (even before we truly understood the meaning of the acronym) began to get us thinking and talking about our next steps. Many grade levels were working to develop common assessments, particularly for units of study in mathematics. In November 2006, the third-grade team decided to take a leap and conduct a Data Team meeting at the end of the multiplication unit. They used the steps outlined in Larry Ainsworth's book *Common Formative Assessments* (2006) to guide them through their first try. They charted the data, with student names, and identified which students were in need of intervention. They discussed how to provide the intervention within their classrooms, set goals for the students, and set a date to reassess. The information gleaned in the Data Team meeting empowered the group. The results were remarkable, and affirming. They were anxious to continue this work.

In January 2007, the teaching staff began to identify essential standards in language arts, mathematics, science, and social studies. We used Ainsworth's *Power Standards* (2003), working first in grade-level teams then school-wide to check for vertical alignment and consistency across grade levels. With this renewed focus, grade levels began to implement more changes within the classrooms. The fifth- and third-grade teams were using the ideas in *Five Easy Steps to a Balanced Math Program* (2000) by Ainsworth and Jan Christinson. They conducted a daily math review in their classrooms, but changed to a grade-level-wide review and weekly quiz. Teachers quickly shared which standards students had mastered and which standards should remain on the review.

As the third-grade team became more comfortable with sharing data, they wrote and received a grant for release time and books. They purchased *Common Formative Assessments* (Ainsworth, 2006), *Power Standards* (Ainsworth, 2003) and *"Unwrapping" the Standards* (Ainsworth, 2003) for each teacher, and spent three full days working on common assessments and data organization. With the seemingly minor changes made in math instruction, standardized test scores increased dramatically that year. Third-grade test scores increased from 37 percent of students proficient to 58 percent as measured by the CST (California Standards Test). Fifth-grade scores increased from 16 percent proficient to 35 percent. This was significant enough to validate the work and motivate us to expand and deepen our Data Teams practices. We knew we were on the right path.

Our work was further refined in the fall of 2007, and throughout the first half of the 2007–2008 school year. We received training from Lisa Almeida, a Professional Development Associate with The Leadership and Learning Center, prior to the start of the school year. The first training focused on "unwrapping" the standards. We became much more aware of the specific skills involved in each of the standards. With a greater understanding of the grade-level expectations, we moved to create better assessments. After "unwrapping" the standards, grade-level teams received differentiated training on the Data Teams process from Lisa Almeida. We continued to receive support from The Leadership and Learning Center and Lisa Almeida throughout the year. This was hard, demanding work that strengthened staff consensus on what we were teaching, what we needed to assess, and what proficiency looked like.

It was the Professional Learning Communities (PLC) Summit in the spring of 2008 that brought the reform process into focus. The four questions: "What do we want our students to learn?"; "How will we know if they have learned it?"; "What will we do if they don't learn it?"; and "What will we do if they already know it?" (DuFour, DuFour, Eaker, Many, 2006) made all of the work of the previous years clear. The book *Learning by Doing* (DuFour, DuFour, Eaker, and Many, 2006) was read by the entire staff, and the phrase became a mantra that continues to be used today. The staff has become entrepreneurial in its practices—searching, testing, assessing, scrapping old practices, and trying out new things. We use data for our decisions, and we know whether a practice has been effective or not. The PLC Summit also helped us to determine next steps, including the development of our Response to Intervention (RTI) model. At that time, we were not quite ready for RTI, but it is now the focus of our work.

There are staff members at Marylin Avenue Elementary School who have taken the lead and changed how we approach new practices. During the 2008–2009 school year, two teachers began reading about The Daily CAFE, (www.thedailycafe.com) and the CAFE strategies (Comprehension, Accuracy, Fluency, and Expanding Vocabulary) that they had developed to organize and focus the teaching and learning of reading. The system includes using assessments to determine individual goals and guide instruction. These teachers shared teaching strategies and their own data with their grade-level team members, who began to implement changes in their classrooms. After using these strategies, the data showed strong increases in reading achievement. By the end of that school year, fourteen staff members registered to go to Portland, Oregon, to be trained in The Daily CAFE system during the summer. The CAFE system has now been adopted school-wide.

With CAFE and our literacy battery, we are now discussing data in regularly scheduled team meetings. This data is used to group students for Tier 2 and Tier 3 intervention in reading. Each grade level analyzes its assessments, organizes the data, meets to discuss the specific intervention strategies, and defines the assessments that will be used to determine the proficiency levels of skills and concepts. We are becoming adept at managing the data and getting a quick turnaround for our intervention groups. Our site data indicates increasing student achievement.

Results

Because of the Data Teams process, our culture, our values and beliefs, and the actions and behaviors of staff members have changed. We've experienced a shift in focus from teacher needs to student needs. Individual students and their instructional needs are now discussed at *every* meeting. Strategies are selected that will help a student evolve. Each week, student progress is reviewed. This collaboration has made every teacher at the table aware of our collective investment in all students at all grade levels.

In addition, the analysis of assessments has led to greater sharing of teaching strategies. By examining data, an individual teacher's success is evident to the team; instructional strategies are shared, to the benefit of all students and teachers. Agreements on essential standards and administration of Common Formative Assessments, based on agreed-upon goals, have enabled access to a common core curriculum for all students. This has created a more equitable learning environment for each of our students. There is a built-in incentive for every teacher to innovate and collaborate so that strategies and techniques for improved learning reach all students.

The work at grade levels has broadened and strengthened our leadership. When an assessment is planned, a discussion takes place about essential standards. This discussion is focused on the calibration of common goals, and then the work begins. One teacher takes on the task of making a draft assessment, which is sent to the others for input and revision. Another makes copies and distributes the assessments, while a third makes charts for recording data. Teachers share the role of leading Data Team meetings, guiding the questions, focusing the discussion, and defining the resulting action items. They also share the role of compiling notes and distributing them to other staff members. Often, staff members outside the grade level will make comments or ask questions about Data Team results. The effectiveness of grade-level teams has led to greater inter-grade level continuity.

The breadth of staff involvement and the sense of shared responsibility at Marylin Avenue Elementary School bring depth to our work. Everyone contributes in ways that are personally comfortable, while each staff member's comfort level is also changing. Staff members who were initially reluctant to take on roles outside their classrooms are getting more involved and taking more risks. This positive climate change occurred over time and continues to be strengthened by a growing

consensus, an expanding body of shared knowledge, and greater commitment to the process of reform. While a few staff members were anxious for a quick change to take place, most remained patient and faithful to the belief that reform is an ongoing process; it is something that will never be quite finished.

For the past year, we have been working to implement a school-wide Data Teams process. As with everything else, this process is continually refined as we make mistakes and see what works. Currently, each grade-level team has set measurable goals for English language arts and math, and has developed specific plans for achieving their goals. Three times a year, we review data from our literacy battery. We review grade-level goals and plans to identify what is and isn't working, to determine if we are on track to achieve our goals, and to make informed decisions regarding the allocation of school resources for intervention.

In addition to cultural changes, and changes in adult actions and behavior, there are many other positive outcomes resulting from our Data Teams implementation. First and most important, we are on track to realize our school mission of increasing achievement for each and every student. From 2006, when we began our Data Teams work, to 2009, student achievement has more than doubled in English language arts and math, not only school-wide, but for every significant subgroup as well. School-wide English language arts scores increased from 24 to 50 percent proficient, and math increased from 30 to 62 percent proficient as measured by the CSTs. In three years, our state Academic Performance Index (API) increased by 129 points. Typically, a year's growth goal is 5–7 points. Considering that our population continues to change, our progress in student achievement is all the more remarkable. As a result of our gains in student achievement, we have exited Program Improvement.

Another positive outcome is that student engagement has greatly increased, and more students take responsibility for their learning. This is visible to anyone who visits our classrooms. Students are on-task, participate in discussions, and work both independently and with small groups. They are eagerly involved in their education. Enthusiasm and energy abound. Attendance has increased from 94 percent to 96.5 percent, suspensions have decreased from 102 to 57 per year, and attendance at parent-teacher conferences has increased from 70 percent to 100 percent.

When we began this journey, our school had the lowest scores of all elementary schools in our district. Most white, middle-class families transferred their children to other schools, and the perception held by the community was that the instruction at our school was poor. As a result of our success, Bay Area newspapers have written articles about our school, we were featured in the National Staff Development Council's Journal of Staff Development (Bernhardt, "Data Driven Decision Making," 2009), and Dr. Victoria Bernhardt wrote the book *Data, Data Everywhere* (2009), chronicling how Marylin Avenue Elementary School uses multiple sources of data for continuous school improvement. Overall, the public's perception of our school has noticeably improved. The wider community is beginning to see our school as a positive learning environment for all students.

Additionally, because of the success we've had in raising student achievement, the school district now regards us as a model learning community for all schools in the district. Our district has decided that all K–12 schools will implement the Data Teams process. This past year, every school identified essential standards. All elementary schools, and two of our middle schools, have been trained in the Data Teams process, and some elementary schools have been trained in writing Common Formative Assessments. There is still much work to be done, but after the first year of implementation of this process, the district API increased 23 points. To put this gain in perspective, the API gains and losses for the three years before that were a 3-point increase, a 5-point loss, and a 7-point increase. Another result of our success has been that many schools both near and far have come to visit and learn from us. Early this year, a large group of superintendents from Alameda County, and the county superintendent, came to tour our school because of our success at increasing achievement for all students.

Walking the halls and breezeways of Marylin Avenue Elementary School, visitors encounter the excitement of learning: eager students engaging in high-level conversations, small and targeted groups meeting at hallway study stations, charts with student achievement data informing the staff of student progress, and anchor charts for instruction adorning the classroom walls.

We have learned that Professional Learning Communities need not lead to "cookie-cutter" classrooms. Our school has not adopted scripted commercial programs as the basis for our reform. Rather, essential standards combined with research-based best practices inform instruction throughout our school. Our teaching staff has been encouraged to experiment with a variety of research-based teaching methods, to collect student performance data, and to analyze the results for effectiveness.

It is of great encouragement to us that our scores have increased substantially since implementing Data Teams three years ago. That there is still much work to be done is humbling. The effects of poverty on our students, the needs of English Language Learners, the increasing achievement levels demanded by the No Child Left Behind legislation, and the added effects of the current economic recession and the resulting cutbacks to schools, are forces we continue to face. Yet, "overwhelmed" is not a label we would adopt for ourselves. Staff members have assumed active and critical leadership roles, and are knowledgeable about the tasks we need to undertake. We remain optimistic that the changes we've made prepare us to match the challenges we'll encounter.

I would like to acknowledge Sharon Abri, Kerry Barger, Sue Carling, Sharon Draggoo, and Marfel Kusko for their contributions to this chapter.

WRITING MY SUCCESS STORY

As you reflect on Marylin Avenue Elementary School's success, take time to think about how their story applies to you in your current setting, and then answer the following questions:

1. *"The 'house was on fire,' and we needed immediate plans and actions to demonstrate improvement, or we would have to face the consequences."*

   Have you ever felt this way? Is the environment you work in more proactive or reactive?

   _____

   _____

   _____

   _____

   _____

2. The author talked frequently about the amount of effort his school put into the improvement process, and the necessity of getting everyone on board. One example: *"This was hard, demanding work that strengthened staff consensus on what we were teaching, what we needed to assess, and what proficiency looked like."*

   Is your staff currently experiencing consensus on what you are teaching, assessing, and what proficiency looks like? If not, what steps can you take to make this more of a reality?

   _____

   _____

   _____

   _____

   _____

3. As a result of Data Teams implementation at Marylin Avenue Elementary School, *"The breadth of staff involvement and the sense of shared responsibility bring depth to our work. Everyone contributes in ways that are personally comfortable, while each staff member's comfort level is also changing."*

Do you work in an environment where everyone contributes and each person has a role he or she is personally comfortable with?

_____

_____

_____

_____

_____

4. *"Another positive outcome is that student engagement has greatly increased, and more students take responsibility for their learning. Students are on-task, participate in discussions, and work both independently and with small groups. They are eagerly involved in their learning."*

What is the direct relationship between intentional and collaborative practices among educators and high levels of student engagement?

_____

_____

_____

_____

_____

SUCCESS STORY EIGHT

Fort Bend Independent School District, Sugar Land, Texas

"At the forefront of change, Fort Bend Independent School District strategically launched Data Teams, focused and highly-structured Professional Learning Communities, as the vehicle to provide focus and drive the change process. Data Teams implementation has become the success story in our district, as the process not only produced visible increases in student achievement, but also brought our focus back to what we value as educators—effective instructional practices that lead to student success and proficiency."

—Olwen E. Herron, Chief Accountability and
Organizational Development Officer

SUCCESSFUL CLIENT:	Fort Bend Independent School District
LOCATION:	Sugar Land, Texas (Urban)
POPULATION:	70,000 students
AUTHOR:	Olwen E. Herron Ed.D., Chief Accountability and Organizational Development Officer

A Data Team in action.

Data Team implementation with integrity.

Fort Bend Independent School District—Then and Now

Fort Bend Independent School District, with almost 70,000 students, is the seventh largest school district in Texas. As a culturally diverse district (Figure 8.1) with a growing student population and more than 90 different dialects and languages spoken by students and their families, the challenges are ongoing. In 2009, however, the school district and all eligible campuses met the Federal No Child Left Behind Act standard of Adequate Yearly Progress (AYP), met all 25 academic indicators in the Texas Accountability System for a "recognized" district, and met or outperformed the state average on all 27 Texas Assessment of Knowledge and Skills (TAKS) tests taken. In addition, 65 percent of Fort Bend campuses earned "exemplary" or "recognized" status in the Texas Accountability System, increasing by nine campuses from 2008. Acknowledging that test results provide only one indicator of whether students are progressing toward mastery of state content standards, it is notable that the percentage of students scoring "proficient" in the core content areas has increased dramatically within a relatively short period of time. Scores in mathematics for African-American, economically disadvantaged, and Hispanic students have risen by 13, 12, and 11 percentage points respectively. Similarly, in science, African-American and economically disadvantaged students' scores have risen by 10 points, and the scores of Hispanic students by 8 points. Gains of up to 9 points are evident in social studies and up to 7 in reading/English

FIGURE 8.1

Fort Bend Independent School District Demographics

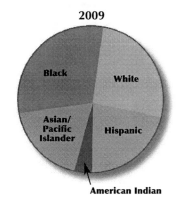

2009

31.42% .... Black
23.71% .... White
23.02% .... Hispanic
21.76% .... Asian/Pacific Islander
0.18% .... American Indian

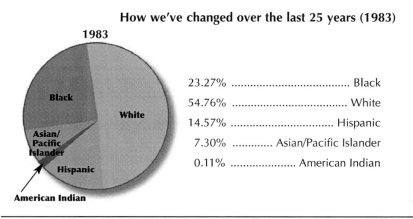

How we've changed over the last 25 years (1983)

1983

23.27% .... Black
54.76% .... White
14.57% .... Hispanic
7.30% .... Asian/Pacific Islander
0.11% .... American Indian

language arts. A detailed review of test scores at the district level over the last three years is provided at the end of this story. Many factors may have contributed to this academic success, but this story will focus on one deliberate change in the way our district does business that has lead to a cultural change in the approach to instruction on its sixty-nine campuses.

Academic success has always been our district's mantra, but instructional practices were not aligned across the district. In 2006–2007, when Dr. Timothy Jenney was appointed as superintendent, twenty-five schools were identified as "underperforming"; within those, ten schools were not making AYP, and eight others were just barely making AYP. In addition, the achievement gap was widening, and test scores were on the decline. The challenge was to raise expectations, sharpen instructional focus, and build internal capacity to provide staff with the resources and tools to meet the challenge.

In the Fort Bend Independent School District, there were pockets of excellence reflective of solid leadership in individual schools, and many excellent teachers working hard to ensure student success. A multitude of instructional programs were in place, and resources were spent annually on educational consultants. There was, however, no instructional focus, alignment of resources, or targeted professional development in place to turn the district around. Instead, the district operated with six faulty practices in place:

1. Campus improvement plans being used as shelf decorations

2. A curriculum aligned with state standards but lacking consistency, rigor, and depth

3. Progress being measured by state test results, but no ongoing formative assessments to measure student proficiency at the classroom level

4. Professional development delivered in one-day events with little expectation for follow-up

5. No district-wide expectation for teachers to collaborate, nor an emphasis on adults taking responsibility for student progress

6. No emphasis on collecting, analyzing, and applying data to drive the instructional process

Without intentional system-wide reform and instructional focus, we could not turn the tide of underperforming schools and low academic achievement. So what is our story? How has our district, with its academically struggling schools, downward trend in student achievement, and a community that had lost faith in the district's ability to deliver a great education, transitioned to one experiencing notable success in such a short time? What are we doing to "move" individuals, campuses, and the whole system forward? We do not claim to have the perfect recipe for change, but we are taking intentional steps to align our instructional vision, resources, and personnel. The Fort Bend Independent School District story is about leadership, a laser-like focus on instruction, high expectations, accountability, capacity-building, purpose-driven work, effective communication, and commitment to staying the course. In fact, our academic profile has changed dramatically in just three years.

At the forefront of change, Fort Bend Independent School District strategically launched Data Teams, focused and highly-structured Professional Learning Communities, as the vehicle to provide focus and drive the change process. Data Teams implementation has become the success story in our district, as the process not only produced visible increases in student achievement, but also brought our focus back to what we value as educators—effective instructional practices that lead to student success and proficiency.

From "Lucky" to "Leading"—A Comprehensive, Long-Term Plan

Fort Bend Independent School District initiated a partnership with The Leadership and Learning Center in September 2007 to apply targeted intervention strategies in twenty-five struggling schools, and to stop the downward spiral in student achievement. The district was dedicated to increasing student achievement through sustained and focused professional development that built on current knowledge and skills. Support from The Center consisted of three major strands: building internal expertise in curriculum development; creating an accountability framework; and implementing Data Teams in low-performing schools as a focused intervention.

In 2007–2008, Making Standards Work and Common Formative Assessments seminars were conducted for the staff, twenty-five of whom were then certified as trainers to deliver the workshops to teacher leaders in all content areas. During 2008–2009, trained teacher leaders and curriculum staff, in turn, "unwrapped" the Power Standards, developed the Big Ideas, wrote the Essential Questions, and created curriculum units and sample Common Formative Assessments. In essence, the curriculum was rewritten, enhanced, and reproduced by internal staff, facilitated by curriculum experts from The Center, as a precursor to the work of Data Teams. In an ideal world, we should have completed the curriculum rewrite, established a district bank of Common Formative Assessments, and then introduced Data-Driven Decision Making. The urgent need for change, however, necessitated that numerous pieces of the puzzle be constructed at the same time, with a plan in place to bring them into alignment within two years.

During the same time frame, a task force developed our District Comprehensive Accountability Framework (DCAF), a holistic accountability plan encompassing District Performance Indicators and Campus Performance Indicators that measure performance and progress toward achieving goals at both levels. The DCAF now serves as the foundation for continuous improvement and makes the leaders in our district accountable for progress. Significantly, Data Teams are referenced in the DCAF as a pivotal strategy for implementing the accountability framework. Data Teams are the vehicles we use for focused analysis of student data from multiple sources; consistent use of Common Formative Assessments to provide timely feedback to students and to inform instruction; and routine teacher collaboration focused on scoring student work, student proficiency, and research-based instructional strategies. Referencing the purpose, process, and strategies for sustaining Data Teams in DCAF effectively linked the work of Data Teams to the district's master plan for success.

In conjunction with this, Data Teams were being implemented at twenty-five high-need campuses. The purpose was to create a paradigm shift from teacher-centered to student-centered learning, and to reinforce the critical role and responsibility of adults in student learning. The following consecutive steps were taken to implement Data Teams in our district:

1. A leadership team of four from each campus, including the principal, data or campus improvement specialist, and at least one core teacher, received professional development in Data-Driven Decision Making and Data Teams.

2. One staff member from each campus received certification training in Data-Driven Decision Making and Data Teams, and would subsequently serve as the resident expert for that campus, lead the training for all staff with the support of the team of four, and assume responsibility for Data Teams implementation in partnership with the campus administrative team.

3. All teachers in the core academic areas received training in Data-Driven Decision Making and Data Teams by the Fort Bend certified trainer.

4. Professional development in Data-Driven Decision Making and Data Teams was followed up with clear expectations about beginning the implementation of Data Teams in support of campus academic goals. For example, if a campus area of weakness and consequent student achievement goal was in mathematics, then a Data Team would be formed first with mathematics teachers.

5. Implementation was immediately followed by four half days of customized support, coaching, and modeling by The Center's professional development associates.

Due to the impact of Data Teams on teacher practice in the first year, all campus administrators were offered the opportunity to work with The Center the next year. An overwhelmingly positive response ensured that the implementation of Data Teams went system-wide in 2008–2009. At this juncture, the same Data Teams implementation steps were taken for all district campuses, and the district created its long-term vision and strategies for change.

Building Capacity and Replicating Success—
The Blueprint for Change

Having piloted Data Teams as an intervention strategy in twenty-five schools with significant buy-in and success, our goals for the 2008–2009 school year were more comprehensive in nature, and were focused on system-wide reform. Upon entering the second year of our partnership with The Center, a blueprint for change was developed to:

- Build capacity in teachers and school leaders through focused professional development.

- Focus on the collection, analysis, and application of data to drive instruction.

- Create a system to ensure accountability at every level of the organization.

- Enhance understanding of the teaching, learning, and leadership strategies behind success.

- Bridge the gap between knowing and doing at every level.

Fort Bend Independent School District's vision for change was under construction, and was deliberately simple in nature. Each year, teachers would receive additional focused professional development to empower them to enhance their instructional practices. The central vehicle for bridging the gap between knowing (professional development) and doing (implementing the learning) would be Data Teams. Professional development training was planned in three phases, each one an essential ingredient in the implementation of effective Data Teams. Each phase starts with targeted professional development providing teachers with

FIGURE 8.2

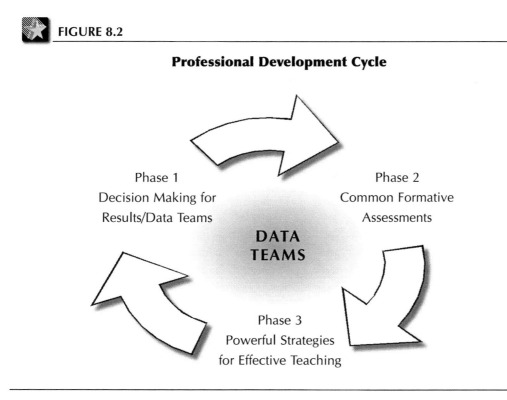

Professional Development Cycle

Phase 1
Decision Making for
Results/Data Teams

Phase 2
Common Formative
Assessments

**DATA
TEAMS**

Phase 3
Powerful Strategies
for Effective Teaching

the knowledge, skills, and tools needed; followed by coaching for implementation and modeling of best practices; and solidified with immediate, ongoing feedback on the level of effective implementation of learning from both certified trainers at each campus and The Center's professional coaches. The cycle of professional development is illustrated in Figure 8.2.

In conjunction with giving teachers the tools for change, campus administrators were provided with the knowledge and skills to lead the implementation. Building leaders experienced all three aforementioned phases of professional development with their staff. In addition, they learned how to coach Data Teams using the implementation rubric, lead change in their schools, and leverage the best practices of teachers to enhance instruction.

Our blueprint for the effective implementation of professional development components over a four-year period is illustrated in Figure 8.3. Highlighted is the focus for each year, followed by internal strategies used to deliver and implement the training provided, and the external support mechanisms that were provided by The Center. External coaching by The Center was deemed essential, as it provided coaching, immediate feedback, and accountability for implementation that could not have been accomplished internally.

The blueprint consists of essential pieces of a puzzle, each one part of a holistic vision to improve student achievement. The foundation for the work was to revise and enhance the curriculum to ensure rigor and alignment with state standards. The vehicle for collaboration and conversations about student proficiency and effective instruction is Data Teams. Embedded within Data Teams, in addition to planning instruction and sharing strategies like the traditional Professional Learning Community model, is a specific Data Teams process that ensures the examination of student data and moves the conversation toward actions to enhance student learning. Common Formative Assessments provide the formative data to examine student progress or student proficiency on a regular basis, and powerful strategies provide the tools teachers need to use to address gaps in student proficiency. We strategically provided the job-embedded ongoing professional development to ensure staff knew how Data Teams operate effectively; what data to analyze, and how to use it to get results; when to use, and how to create, a variety of quality formative assessments; and what research-based instructional strategies to use to teach the concepts and eliminate the gaps in student performance. Without the pieces in place and internal capacity developed, it would have been difficult for significant change to occur.

 **FIGURE 8.3**

Blueprint for Change

Year	Professional Development Initiative	Internal Strategies for Delivering Training, Building Capacity, and Implementing Data Teams	Coaching, Support, and Feedback
One	*Data Teams (DT) and Data-Driven Decision Making (DDDM)*	1. Certification training in DT and DDDM conducted by The Center for internal district trainers and campus-level specialists 2. DT and DDDM training delivered to core teams of 4 at each campus 3. DT and DDDM training provided to all staff at each campus by certified internal trainers 4. DT and DDDM implemented at the campus level in core subject areas	Individualized campus coaching—4 visits per year per campus
Two	*Common Formative Assessments (CFAs)*	1. Certification training in CFAs conducted by The Center for internal district trainers and campus-level specialists 2. CFAs training delivered by The Center to core teams of 4 at each campus 3. CFAs training provided to all staff at each campus by certified internal trainers 4. CFAs training implemented in Data Teams	Individualized campus coaching—2–4 visits per year, focused on CFAs/Data Teams implementation and differentiated according to need Support seminars on DT and DDDM for certified internal trainers
Three	*Powerful Strategies for Effective Teaching-I (PSET-Part I)*	1. Certification training in PSET-Part I conducted by The Center for internal district trainers and campus-level specialists 2. PSET-Part I training on 3–4 specific strategies provided to all staff at each campus by certified internal trainers 3. Specific strategies (3–4) from PSET-Part I training implemented in Data Teams	Individualized campus coaching—2–4 visits per year, focused on CFAs/Data Teams implementation and differentiated according to need Support seminars on DT, DDDM, and CFAs for certified internal trainers
Four	*Powerful Strategies for Effective Teaching-II (PSET-Part II)*	1. Additional training in PSET-Part II on 3–4 more specific strategies provided by certified internal trainers for each campus 2. Specific strategies (3–4) from PSET-Part II training implemented in Data Teams	Individualized coaching, differentiated according to need Support seminars on DT, DDDM, CFAs, and PSET Parts I and II for certified internal trainers

> *"What's really fascinating is that teachers are spending quality time deciding which instructional strategy would be best for students to achieve mastery of the content."*
>
> MATH INSTRUCTIONAL SPECIALIST

From Isolation to Collaboration with Purpose—Beyond PLCs

When teachers begin to collaborate about student proficiency and instruction and share their expertise with each other, transformation takes place. Data Teams are Fort Bend Independent School District's Professional Learning Communities, but with substance and "teeth" (a data analysis process)—they create a laser-like focus on instruction and student proficiency. As one of our principals states: "We found that although PLCs provided the structure, it was actually Data Teams that provided the process necessary to impact student achievement on our campus."

Implementing Data Teams in the district not only established a scheduled time for teachers to meet with other teachers, but also provided a substantive reason for the meeting. There are expected outcomes, and an official record of decisions made in Data Team meetings. Our teachers no longer work in isolation in their individual classrooms, but work together as teams sharing common assessments, identifying effective instructional strategies for student success, and analyzing student work and data in a systematic manner.

> *"Being able to openly share ideas and strategies, as well as struggles we might be experiencing, has helped us grow as educators."*
>
> FOURTH-GRADE DATA TEAM LEADER

Initially, teachers were intimidated, reluctant to share practices, and fearful of discussing and analyzing their student data with peers. However, after positive reinforcement and understanding of the highly-structured process in place, teachers became open to collaboration as the norm. Interestingly, one Fort Bend teacher with over twenty years of experience, after initial resistance to Data Team meetings, proclaimed it was the best professional development she had ever had, because it was an incredible opportunity to learn from her peers.

> *"I had not seen true teacher collaboration until we implemented Data Teams."*
>
> ELEMENTARY PRINCIPAL

With the implementation of Data Teams comes individual accountability. Teachers are accountable to their peers, because the data reflects not only the proficiency level of the students, but also the effectiveness of the teachers. As one of our district data specialists suggests, "The Data Team concept embraces the 'it takes a village' notion in the school context, as teachers help each other meet the needs of all students in their grade level." When operating effectively, the data analysis is not about the teacher's pedagogy, but what the team can learn from each other to ensure the success of all students. Data Teams move teachers beyond weekly lesson planning to reflective teaching, and, as such, become an example of job-embedded, relevant, focused professional development at its best.

> *"The results have made our teachers into believers in the Data Teams process."*
>
> MIDDLE SCHOOL PRINCIPAL

Principals and assistant principals play a vital role in the success of Data Teams implementation in Fort Bend Independent School District. Where Data Teams are most effective, the principal and building leadership team are participating in and monitoring the work. Celebration of success and recognition of improvement are paramount. One middle school principal credits Data Teams with being the systematic approach that led to improved achievement on state standardized tests and local assessments. Teachers collaboratively plan and make data-driven decisions about instructional strategies after reviewing in detail the pre- and post-assessments. Of course, without positive outcomes, it would be difficult to keep the momentum going.

Interestingly, the Data Teams process also allows students to take an active role in monitoring their progress—they are able to track their growth through data walls and monitor their scores on post-assessments in their core classes. Data walls are a feature of both elementary and secondary campuses, and make the work of Data Teams a reality for students. Figure 8.4 shows sample data walls from both the elementary and secondary levels.

The overarching purpose of Data Teams becomes clear when the teams' goals are clearly linked to campus improvement goals. When viewed as a positive strategy to achieve campus goals and address areas of weakness, buy-in is stronger.

> *"Students are active participants in the Data Teams process. Before the implementation of Data Teams, assessments were a Friday routine. Today, Common Formative Assessments are a vehicle for instruction."*
>
> MIDDLE SCHOOL CAMPUS IMPROVEMENT SPECIALIST

Fort Bend's School Improvement Plan template was redesigned as part of creating the

 **FIGURE 8.4**

Data Walls

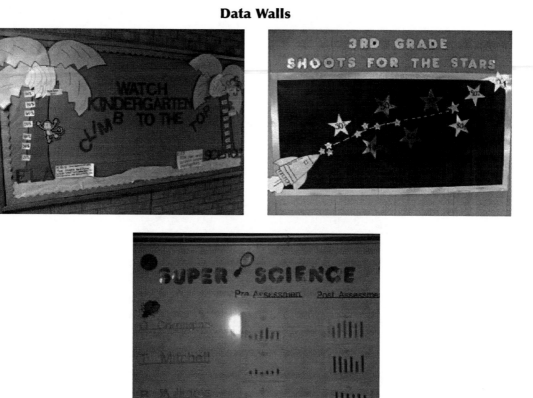

comprehensive accountability framework, or CAF. The template now incorporates three distinct phases in working toward achieving goals: planning, implementing, and monitoring progress. Significantly, the same emphasis on adult actions leading to results inherent in the Data Teams process underpins the PIM™ Continuous Improvement Process (Figure 8.5).

> *"Data Teams are the answer to goal setting, progress monitoring, and goal achieving."*
>
> ELEMENTARY DATA SPECIALIST

Within the template, campuses select two academic goals related to areas of weakness, and these areas become the focus of the Data Teams. Ultimately, the goal is for the campus as a whole, and teachers and principals individually, to understand why they are getting results. As Doug Reeves demonstrates in the Leadership for Learning Framework (Reeves, 2006, p. 6), leaders must understand the antecedents

⭐ **FIGURE 8.5**

PIM™ Continuous Improvement Process

MONITOR

Reflect and plan on future actions
- Analyze expected and actual outcomes/results against targets
- Complete evaluation cycle with reflections and plans for the future

Monitor progress
- Develop a monitoring plan including what, who, and when
- Include monitoring frequency

MONITOR
Ensure accurate implementaton and effectiveness of the plan

PLAN
Identify critical areas, goals, and strategies for improving student achievement/performance

IMPLEMENT
Implement plan to improve student achievement/performance

PLAN

Identify critical needs
- Collect and organize data necessary for analysis
- Identify critical areas for improving performance

Develop a plan
- Use identified critical needs to drive plan
- Use inquiry process to identify cause and effect relationships
- Set goals that are specific, measurable, achievable, relevant, and timely

IMPLEMENT
- Target research-based strategies/best practices
- Design implementation with action steps and timelines
- Select professional development
- Develop stakeholder involvement plan

of excellence, so that they may be replicated to achieve results. Our district is using the PIM™ Continuous Improvement Process district-wide; consequently, planning, implementation, and monitoring are the norm at every level. Data Teams have shown that this model works at the individual classroom level and at the campus level through the School Improvement Plan, therefore, why not implement it in other areas? Prior to Data Teams and the PIM™ process, the missing piece in strategic planning and in implementing new initiatives in our district was monitoring for results. These strategies have moved the district from planning and knowing what to do to actually doing it and monitoring progress.

Data Teams in Fort Bend do not operate in isolation, but are a moving piece in the instructional process. As demonstrated in Figure 8.6, they are placed deliberately in the middle of the instructional cycle. This model illustrates how all of the instructional pieces fit together. At the outset in 2008, our district curriculum was realigned with the state standards and Power Standards were identified. Subsequently, the Power Standards were "unwrapped," and the Big Ideas and Essential Questions established. This work created the foundation for the work of

 **FIGURE 8.6**

The Fort Bend Independent School District Standards-Assessment Alignment Diagram

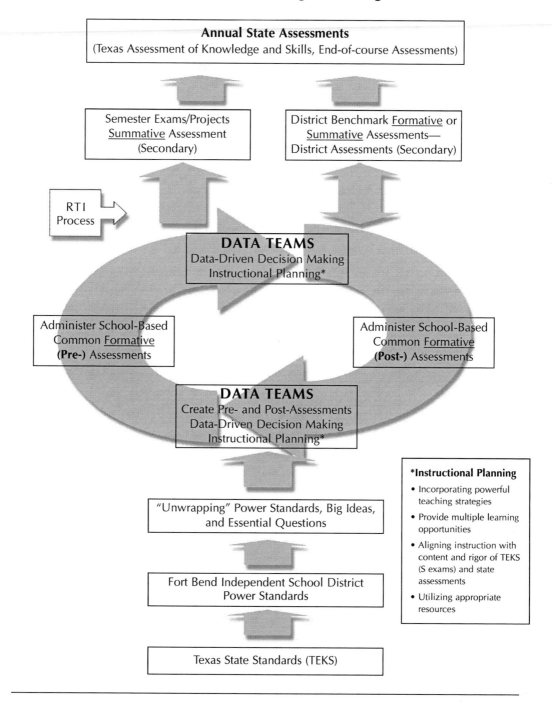

the Data Teams as illustrated by its placement at the bottom of Figure 8.6. Within the Data Teams cycle, and illustrated in the middle of the diagram, instructional planning takes place using the Power Standards that we identified. We plan content units, create lessons, and write pre- and post-assessments based on the Power Standards. Common Formative Assessments are administered; data is analyzed, and the cycle of instruction starts again.

The work of Data Teams is ongoing, and the continuous loop repeats itself in each unit of instruction to continuously assess if students are mastering what is being taught. Notably, semester examinations, district benchmark tests, and annual state assessments provide important summative data, but these are not the data resources used to inform instruction in the classroom on a weekly or daily basis; therefore, the Data Teams process has filled the data void in the instructional process. As one elementary principal said, "The use of real data from Common Formative Assessments enables teachers to specifically target their instruction to meet the needs of their students."

"What You Monitor Gets Done!"—Strategies for Sustainability

Sustainability and deep implementation are crucial in planning and implementing any initiative; therefore, intentional strategies must be in place from the outset. We adopted several methods to sustain the implementation of our Data Teams across the district.

First, the decision was made to invest in certifying teacher leaders and data and campus improvement specialists to teach The Center seminars within the district. Certifying our own trainers has built internal capacity, ensured deeper under-standing of the seminar concepts, created buy-in, and provided teacher leaders with new tools to support other educators at the campus level. District staff members are certified in Making Standards Work (now titled Engaging Classroom Assess-ments), Data-Driven Decision Making (now titled Decision Making for Results), Data Teams, Common Formative Assessments, and Powerful Strategies for Effective Teaching. In addition, personnel certified in Data-Driven Decision Making, Common Formative Assessments, and Powerful Strategies are strategically placed on every campus to serve as resident experts in support of the Data Teams. Certified specialists are responsible for collecting Data Team minutes from team leaders, serving as the liaison with campus administration, coaching educators on the Data Teams process, ensuring collaboration on creating Common Formative Assessments based on the standards, and sharing effective instructional strategies to address the gaps in learning.

> *"When the focus shifts to things that they can control, teachers are empowered. Teachers can adjust their teaching, refine their assessments, and be positive role models for their students. In that sense, the Data Teams process develops teacher efficacy."*
>
> ELEMENTARY DATA SPECIALIST

One notable strategy for sustainability has been the support, feedback, and ongoing accountability brought through coaching and implementation visits by The Center staff. Differentiated coaching and modeling based on the needs of individual campuses, and instant feedback using a comprehensive implementation rubric were instrumental in creating forward momentum. We credit sustainability to the professional coaching connected to specific goals and needs, specifically focused on Data Teams implementation. Preparing for visits, providing evidence of teams in action, and demonstrating progress between coaching sessions provided motivation for our campus staff and administrators.

Involving the assistant superintendents for elementary, middle, and high schools in monitoring the level of implementation of Data Teams has also been an effective strategy for sustainability. Regular meetings take place with The Center coaches and the assistant superintendents to review the progress of each campus, share success stories and barriers to implementation, and brainstorm ways to move the system forward. Significantly, assistant superintendents regularly attend Data Team meetings at their assigned campuses to show support and monitor progress, thus setting clear district expectations for implementation.

Communicating expectations over and over is foundational to sustainability. Since the inception of Data Teams in our district, campuses have dedicated one campus professional development day annually to the work of Data Teams. There is also a clear expectation that campus administrators will attend Data Team meetings and become involved in the conversations about instruction that ensue.

Evaluating progress plays a significant role in sustainability. The Center's semester report detailing the level of implementation of campus Data Teams provides one source of valuable data about implementation at the campus level, while analysis of the results of an annual Data Team survey provides information from Data Team members (teachers) and administration on the perceived level of implementation and barriers to success. The district's survey asks specific questions to assess if teachers believe Data Team meetings are being held regularly, are focused, and have specific goals. Other questions inquire about the level of support of building administrators and whether they are engaged and participate in Data Team meetings. In addition, teachers are asked to assess their level of understanding and comfort with various aspects of their Data Team's work, such as analysis of assessment data, development of specific and measurable goals, creation of common assessments, scoring common assessments, examination of student work to identify strengths and weaknesses, and ascertaining if the goals were achieved to determine next steps. In May 2009, a third section was added to the survey that focuses on the impact of Data Teams on various aspects of teacher practice. A copy of the survey questions is included at the end of this chapter. Currently underway is an analysis of the level of implementation of Data Teams assessed utilizing The Center rubric and its relation to increased student achievement on specific campuses. Data from these sources is used to make improvements and address issues with implementation.

In May 2008, our first Data Teams implementation survey was administered to forty teachers at twenty-five schools who were implementing Data Teams for the first time, with a teacher return rate of 66 percent. In May 2009, the same survey questions, with one added section, were administered online to teachers at all Fort Bend Independent School District campuses. Figure 8.7 shows the results of a section of the survey that highlights teacher perception of the impact of Data Teams on various aspects of their teaching.

Notably, over 70 percent of our teachers believe Data Teams have had a moderate or high impact on their collaboration with colleagues, meeting individual student needs, increasing the rigor of instruction, using assessments to modify instruction, and implementing new instructional strategies. The majority of respondents of the survey are in their first year of implementation of Data Teams. As all schools have now implemented Data Teams to some extent, the data will

FIGURE 8.7

Data Teams Implementation Survey Part 3

Area of Impact	No Impact	Limited Impact	Moderate Impact	High Impact
Implementation of new teaching strategies	7.8% (123)	20.6% (323)	**46.9% (737)**	24.6% (387)
Collaboration with colleagues on pacing	6.9% (108)	14.6% (228)	**41.8% (654)**	36.7% (575)
Collaboration with colleagues on instructional practices	7.1% (110)	14.4% (225)	**40.3% (629)**	38.2% (595)
Differentiating instruction to meet individual student needs	7.7% (119)	18.1% (282)	**42.8% (665)**	31.4% (488)
Rigor of classroom assessment	7.5% (118)	18.0% (282)	**47.6% (744)**	26.8% (419)
Modifying instruction based on assessment results	6.5% (101)	16.9% (263)	**42.7% (665)**	34.0% (529)

serve as district-wide baseline data on Data Teams implementation and its impact on professional practice. Preliminary results suggest that a change in the practice of teachers in this district is in progress.

"This Too Shall Pass"—Changing Our Culture and Envisioning Next Steps

Sustainability and accountability will lead to a change in culture over time. As one veteran teacher says as she acknowledges that Data Teams have transformed the daily practice of teachers in a positive manner, "We cannot go back now." Part of the reason for the growing acceptance of this new instructional focus and change in practice is that the expectations are the same for all campuses across the district. Dr. Jenney's purpose has been to align the arrows and move Fort Bend Independent School District away from being a system of schools and toward being one school system with a clear instructional focus. As teachers communicate with one another from campus to campus, it becomes obvious that the direction is the same and a common language is being spoken. Conversations about Data Teams, Common Formative Assessments, high-yield strategies, and student proficiency are becoming the norm; therefore, momentum is building as our district evolves into a system moving in one direction.

> *"Our goal is to move from being a system of schools to a school system."*
>
> SUPERINTENDENT

Taking time to celebrate success is also reinforcing our new instructional practices. Recognizing increases in student achievement at administrative team meetings, sharing academic successes with the community, and working in partnership with The Center to produce a DVD series on effective Data Teams are only the beginning. Recognition is given to effective teams by having them model the Data Teams process for other teams across the district. Effective teams have been recorded and used in district training to model good practice and indirectly generate positive competition among campuses.

Undoubtedly, the joy is in the journey, and we have certainly not arrived, but continue to seek the means to keep our momentum going forward by anticipating the next steps on our journey toward excellence. Continuing to communicate expectations and monitor implementation, as well as continuing to build the capacity of staff involved, are paramount. Today, every campus is utilizing the Decision Making for Results process in its Data Teams to drive instructional decisions. There are model campuses utilizing Data Teams in every core area and at every level with complete teacher buy-in; and others, though still in the throes of early implementation, are beginning to gain traction. The goal is to sustain the effort and embed the process in our culture. Consequently, all schools will have Data Teams consistently reviewing and analyzing data and using the results to drive instruction at all levels.

This grassroots effort, which began with teachers collaborating and using data to drive instruction, also has potential for other parts of our district. Next steps include implementing a department improvement plan to focus on adult actions with special emphasis on collection, analysis and application of data to show results, and implementing Data Teams at the department and district level. In many respects, the journey is just beginning, as there is much more exciting work to do.

Upon reflection, changing the culture and the way business is conducted on a daily basis is very hard work. Creating quality Common Formative Assessments, analyzing data, sharing effective strategies, and consistently monitoring student progress all demand focus and energy. However, the rewards far surpass the demands of the work when students with the greatest needs receive quality instruction in their areas of weakness and achieve academically. When teachers collaborate, take responsibility for student learning, and constantly work to improve their practice, results will follow. When building leaders lead by example, set goals that stretch their staff, and participate in Data Team conversations about instruction and student proficiency, whole campuses move forward together. When central office leaders implement Data Teams with fidelity, provide adequate professional development and support, and monitor for results, changes in culture and practice occur that drive student achievement.

Districts must find high-leverage practices to unleash powerful consequences and, undoubtedly, effective Data Teams is one of those practices. Our challenge to those who read this story is to review the evidence; invest in results-driven, ongoing, job-embedded professional development; and establish the foundation for continued professional growth and student success.

FIGURE 8.8

Fort Bend Independent School District
Texas Assessment of Knowledge & Skills (TAKS), 2006 to 2009

Performance Results	2006* Percent Met Standard	2007** Percent Met Standard	2008† Percent Met Standard	2009‡ Percent Met Standard	Change From 2008 to 2009
Reading/English Language Arts					
All Students	90%	91%	93%	94%	+4%
African American	85%	86%	89%	91%	+6%
Hispanic	84%	85%	88%	89%	+5%
White	97%	97%	98%	98%	+1%
Economically Disadvantaged	81%	83%	86%	88%	+7%
Mathematics					
All Students	77%	79%	83%	85%	+8%
African American	61%	64%	70%	74%	+13%
Hispanic	67%	69%	75%	78%	+11%
White	91%	91%	94%	95%	+4%
Economically Disadvantaged	63%	66%	71%	75%	+12%
Writing					
All Students	94%	93%	93%	94%	0%
African American	90%	89%	90%	92%	+2%
Hispanic	90%	90%	90%	90%	0%
White	98%	97%	97%	97%	–1%
Economically Disadvantaged	89%	87%	88%	90%	+1%
Science					
All Students	76%	76%	78%	82%	+6%
African American	60%	60%	64%	70%	+10%
Hispanic	63%	64%	68%	71%	+8%
White	91%	92%	92%	94%	+3%
Economically Disadvantaged	58%	60%	63%	68%	+10%
Social Studies					
All Students	91%	91%	94%	95%	+4%
African American	85%	85%	90%	92%	+7%
Hispanic	82%	84%	90%	91%	+9%
White	97%	98%	98%	99%	+2%
Economically Disadvantaged	81%	82%	88%	90%	+9%

* 2006 AEIS Standard Accountability Indicator   ** 2007 AEIS Standard Accountability Indicator
† 2008 AEIS Standard Accountability Indicator   ‡ 2009 AEIS Standard Accountability Indicator

AEIS (Academic Excellence Indicator System) is an annual report providing information on the performance of students in each school and district in Texas.

FIGURE 8.9

Fort Bend Independent School District
Data-Driven Decision Making/Data Teams Implementation

Survey Questions

The following questions about the actual Data Team meetings held were answered with 1 (*strongly disagree*); 2 (*disagree*); 3 (*undecided*); 4 (*agree*); or 5 (*strongly agree*):

1. Data Team meetings are scheduled and consistently held on a regular basis.

2. Meetings begin and end on time.

3. Data Team members are present, on task, and come prepared with all needed materials or data.

4. Minutes are taken, reflecting the content of the meeting, and are distributed to everyone.

5. Teacher input is done in a respectful and open environment. Data Team members participate in focused discussions. Members feel valued.

6. Discussions are based on student work, common assessment results, and strategies to improve student achievement.

7. Interruptions or distractions seldom occur.

8. There is a goal for the meetings to reach consensus, to set the next agenda, and to assign needed tasks and timelines for the next meeting.

9. There is understanding and general agreement that products produced or decisions made will be evaluated to determine effectiveness and future use.

10. Building administrators are engaged in and supportive of Data Teams.

The following questions about teacher perceptions of the work involved in the Data Teams process were answered with 1 (*having difficulty*); 2 (*progressing*); 3 (*proficient*); or 4 (*highly developed*):

1. Analyzing district /common assessment data to identify student achievement strengths and weaknesses

2. Developing a SMART goal (specific, measurable, achievable, relevant, and timely) that is targeted at a particular area of weakness

3. Discussing and brainstorming ways to more effectively teach to an area of weakness and implementing the new strategy

4. Creating/identifying a common assessment to administer at the conclusion of the teaching time

5. Locating appropriate materials from which to create common assessments

6. Administering and scoring a common assessment

7. Agreeing on what constitutes proficiency on common assessments

8. Examining student work to identify strengths and obstacles

9. Examining team data and analyzing results

10. If the SMART goal was achieved, determining the next most urgent area of weakness that has been identified

11. Establishing the date, time, and location of the next Data Team meeting

The following questions about the impact of Data Teams in each of these areas of teaching were answered with 1 (*no impact*); 2 (*limited impact*); 3 (*moderate impact*); or 4 (*high impact*):

1. Implementation of new strategies

2. Collaboration with colleagues on pacing

3. Collaboration with colleagues on instructional practices

4. Differentiating instruction to meet individual student needs

5. Rigor of classroom assessment

6. Modifying instruction based on assessment results

Fourth-grade data wall.

The Work of Data Teams in Fort Bend Independent School District

Seventh-grade social studies data wall.
Lighter bars = pre-test
Darker bars = post-test

Modeling a research-based strategy.

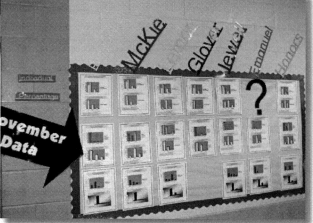

Administrators and specialists observation data wall: teaching strategies observed and then discussed in Data Teams.

WRITING MY SUCCESS STORY

As you reflect on the success of Fort Bend Independent School District, take time to think about how their story applies to you in your current setting, and then answer the following questions:

1. *"Instead, the district operated with six faulty practices in place:*

    1. Campus improvement plans being used as shelf decorations

    2. A curriculum aligned with state standards but lacking consistency, rigor, and depth

    3. Progress being measured by state test results, but no ongoing formative assessments to measure student proficiency at the classroom level

    4. Professional development delivered in one-day events with little expectation for follow-up

    5. No district-wide expectation for teachers to collaborate, nor an emphasis on adults taking responsibility for student progress

    6. No emphasis on collecting, analyzing, and applying data to drive the instructional process."

    Out of the six faulty practices described above, which one resonates with you in your current setting?

    _____

    _____

    _____

    _____

    _____

2. *"The central vehicle for bridging the gap between knowing (professional development) and doing (implementing the learning) would be Data Teams."*

> As the author recognizes, often a gap exists between what we know to be effective practices, and what we choose to implement. Where are you in this journey? How would you rate your team, school, and district?

_____

_____

_____

_____

_____

3. *"Taking time to celebrate success is also reinforcing our new instructional practices. Recognizing increases in student achievement at administrative team meetings, sharing academic successes with the community, and working in partnership with The Center to produce a DVD series on effective Data Teams are only the beginning. Recognition is given to effective teams by having them model the Data Teams process for other teams across the district. Effective teams have been recorded and used in district training to model good practice and indirectly generate positive competition among campuses."*

> It is clear this author believes in the power of ongoing celebration as an essential part of the Data Teams process. What are you currently celebrating at your school or district? Are the celebrations based on both cause and effect data?

_____

_____

_____

_____

_____

Conclusion

*"There is no greater agony than
bearing an untold story inside you."*
—Maya Angelou

It has been said that the mere existence of a story does not create a culture; rather, it is the deliberate decision to take action and *retell* the compelling tale that leaves a lasting impact.

Just as a community's culture can be established by the stories its people tell and retell, a school's culture can be created and carried on through the selective choice of which stories are told within the four walls of each building, and retold to the community and colleagues within the industry. We tell stories to leave our mark on the world, to leave a legacy for generations to come. Each one of us has an authentic tale to tell, and each of us will have more tales to tell in the future.

It is critical that teachers, administrators, and district leaders hear, consume, and respond to these stories. We must be poised to generate a response to the stories we hear, and to disrupt counterproductive responses whenever necessary. We must be aware of the stories being told, observe how the people around us respond to them, and be ready and willing to intervene when necessary. In complex environments like school systems, if you want to change the culture of a group, you can start by changing the response to the stories being told within it.

What story will you continue to tell in your school and district? Better yet, what stories have you heard that you will choose to act upon? Will you tell a story that is defined by external factors (parents, legislation, budget cuts, the media, etc.), or one that is directed by decisive action, and that results in dramatic gains in student achievement?

Hopefully, the accounts in the previous pages have inspired you to take action, to make mid-course corrections, to take a different path, and to look deeply at your own story. Our students and communities deserve nothing less than our best efforts to look at the data from our schools, make inferences based on those data, determine strategies to meet the needs that the data bring to light, and monitor the results of our strategies. This is the Data Teams process, and it is a story that has transformed, and will continue to transform, school cultures. It is a story that will be told for generations to come.

References

Ainsworth, L. B. (2003). *"Unwrapping" the standards: A simple process to make standards manageable.* Englewood, CO: Lead + Learn Press.

Ainsworth, L. B. (2003). *Power standards: Identifying the standards that matter the most.* Englewood, CO: Lead + Learn Press.

Ainsworth, L., & Christinson, J. (2000). *Five easy steps to a balanced math program: A practical guide for K–8 classroom teachers.* Alexandria, VA: ASCD.

Ainsworth, L. B., & Viegut, D. J. (2006). *Common formative assessments: How to connect standards-based instruction and assessment.* Thousand Oaks, CA: Corwin Press.

Allaire, Y., & Firsirotu, M. E. (1984). Theories of organizational culture. *Organization Studies, 5,* pp. 193–226.

Becker, H. S., & Geer, B. (1960). Latent culture. *Administrative Science Quarterly, 5,* pp. 303–313.

Bernhardt, V. (2009). *Data, data everywhere.* Larchmont, NY: Eye on Education.

Bernhardt, V. (2009). Data-driven decision making. *Journal of staff development.* vol. 30, no. 1. National Staff Development Council.

Collins, J. (2001). *Good to great: Why some companies make the leap...and others don't.* New York: HarperBusiness.

Danielson, C. (1996). *Enhancing professional practice: A framework for teaching.* Alexandria, VA: ASCD.

Downey, C., English, F. W., & Steffy, B. (2004). *The three-minute classroom walk-through: Changing school supervisory practice one teacher at a time.* Thousand Oaks, CA: Corwin.

DuFour, R., DuFour, R., Eaker, R., & Many, T. (2006). *Learning by doing: A handbook for professional learning communities at work.* Bloomington, IN: Solution Tree.

DuFour, R., & Eaker, R. (1998). *Professional learning communities at work: Best practices for enhancing student achievement.* Bloomington, IN: Solution Tree.

Louis, M. R. (1980). Organizations as culture-bearing milieux. In L. R. Pondy, et al. (Eds.) *Organizational symbolism.* Greenwich, CT: JAI.

Marzano, R. (2009). *Tracking student progress and scoring scales.* Retrieved February 21, 2010 from www.marzanoresearch.com/research/strategy20_trackingprogress.aspx

Reeves, D. B. (2009). *Leading change in your school: How to conquer myths, build commitment, and get results.* Alexandria, VA: ASCD.

Reeves, D. B. (2006). *The learning leader: How to focus school improvement for better results.* Alexandria, VA: ASCD.

Reeves, D. B. (2002). *Making standards work, 3rd ed.: How to implement standards-based assessments in the classroom, school, and district.* Englewood, CO: Lead + Learn Press.

Reeves, D. B. (2002). *The daily disciplines of leadership: How to improve student achievement, staff motivation, and personal organization.* San Francisco: Jossey-Bass.

Reeves, D. B. (2000). *Accountability in action: A blueprint for learning organizations.* Englewood, CO: Lead + Learn Press.

Reeves, D. B. (2000). The 90/90/90 schools: A case study. In D. B. Reeves, *Accountability in action: A blueprint for learning organizations* (pp. 185–208). Englewood, CO: Lead + Learn Press.

Sanborn, M. (2008). *The encore effect: How to achieve remarkable performance in anything you do.* New York: The Doubleday Publishing Group.

Schmoker, M. J. (2006). *Results now: How we can achieve unprecedented improvements in teaching and learning.* Alexandria, VA: ASCD.

The Leadership and Learning Center (2010). *Data teams, 3rd ed.* Englewood, CO: Lead + Learn Press.

The Leadership and Learning Center (2008). *Decision making for results.* Englewood, CO: Lead + Learn Press.

Trice, H. M., &. Beyer, J. M. (1993). *Cultures of work organizations.* Englewood Cliffs, NJ: Prentice Hall.

Notes

Notes

Notes

Notes